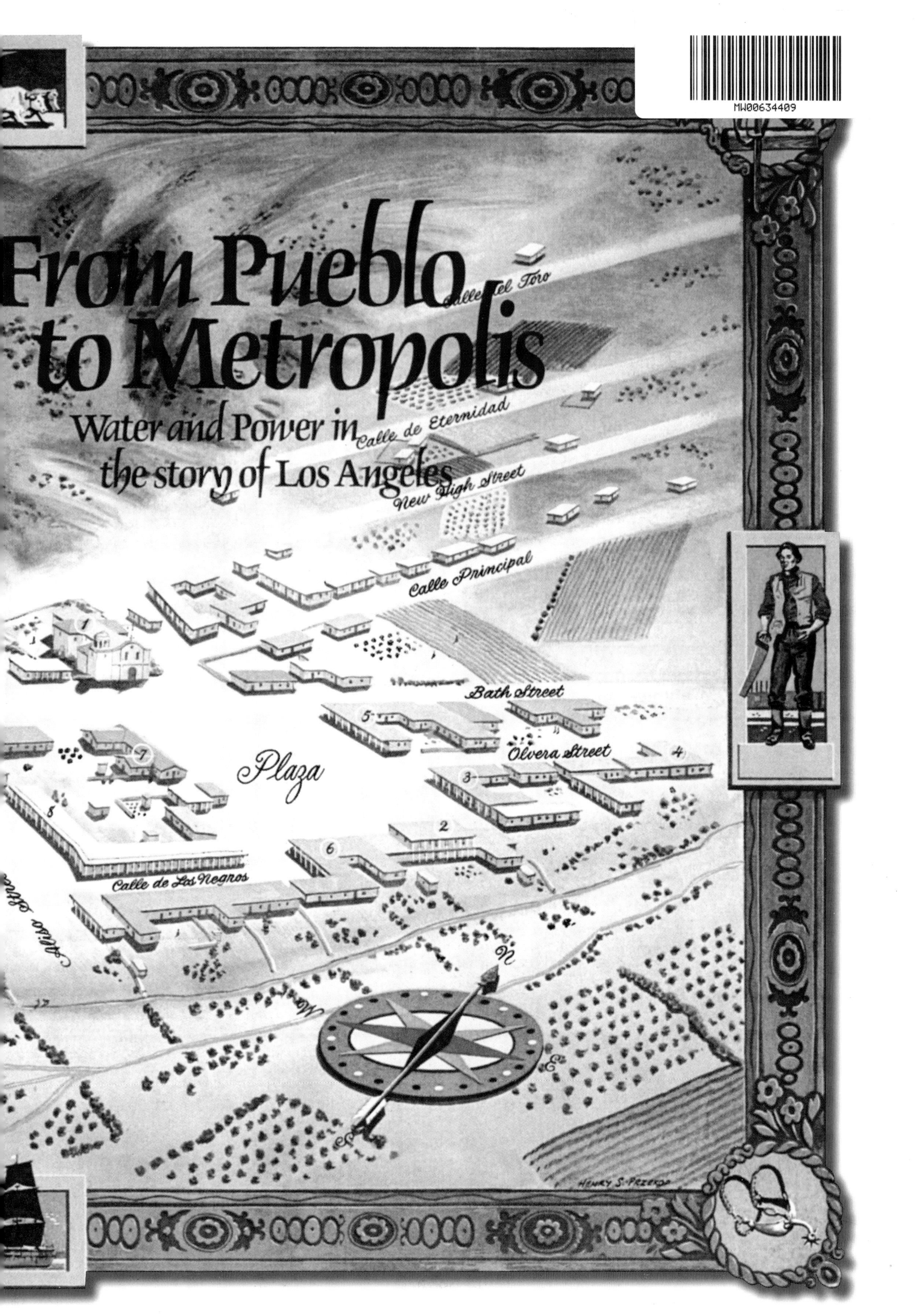
From Pueblo to Metropolis
Water and Power in the story of Los Angeles
Calle del Toro
Calle de Eternidad
New High Street
Calle Principal
Bath Street
Olvera Street
Plaza
Calle de Los Negros
Aliso Street
N
HENRY S. PRZEKOP
MW00634409

LAFD — Land, Sea & Air

A Pictorial History of the Los Angeles City Fire Department

M.T. Publishing Company, Inc.
P.O. Box 6802
Evansville, Indiana 47719-6802
www.mtpublishing.com

The materials were compiled and produced using available information. M.T. Publishing Company, Inc., and the Los Angeles City Fire Department Historical Society & Museum regret they cannot assume liability for errors or omissions.

Graphic Designer:
Alena L. Richards Kiefer

Library of Congress Control Number:
2006932311

ISBN: 1-932439-57-9

Printed in the
United States of America

Table of Contents

DEDICATION

In 1986 Paul Ditzel wrote a complete history of the Los Angeles Fire Department. It was a valuable source of information for us while we were researching the history of the department. Paul wrote what is considered the most comprehensive and most accurate book ever written on the LAFD.

He was widely acclaimed as the "dean" of fire service authors and in his lifetime wrote 15 books and over 600 articles for magazines. He was a contributing editor to *Firehouse Magazine* and a former contributing editor to *Fire Engineering*. His best selling book, *Fire Engines, Firefighting* was submitted for a Pulitzer Prize in American History.

He held a Master of Science Degree from Northwestern University where he graduated with highest scholastic honors.

In 1967 he was appointed as the Los Angeles Fire Department's first civilian fire inspector.

We are in no way trying to (or would be able to) meet the stature and excellence of his fine book. We regret that Paul Ditzel passed away recently and we are unable to thank him in person for the help his writings gave to us.

Thank you Paul.

Paul C. Ditzel
1926-2005

From the office of the Fire Chief....

FOREWARD

Since the first Los Angeles Fire Chief, Charles E. Miles, was elected Chief Engineer of the Los Angeles Fire Department (LAFD) in 1876, a great many historic events have enriched the LAFD. Historically, the department is known for being the first to utilize numerous innovative procedures and methods in fire fighting which have been and are still adopted by fire departments throughout the world.

In 1995, I had the honor of being appointed the Fire Chief of the greatest fire department in the country. Since the department was officially established in 1886, the city has evolved from a small horse and buggy town to a vast area of over 469 square miles. The LAFD provides fire protection and emergency medical services to immense areas ranging from high-rise office and apartment complexes, sprawling brush areas, a major harbor and two of the world's busiest airports.

This year, the LAFD is celebrating its 120th year of service to the citizens of Los Angeles. To mark this event, the members of the Los Angeles Fire Department's Historical Society have been inspired to produce this book to capture in photographs some of those historic events.

It is my pleasure to present this book to all who are interested in the history of the LAFD, whether they are members of the fire department or those who simply have an interest in the profession of fire fighting. Please join us in reliving some of the historic events of the LAFD - On Land, Sea & Air.

William R. Bamattre

Fire Chief William R. Bamattre
Los Angeles Fire Department

INTRODUCTION

Founded in October of 1982, the Los Angeles Fire Department Historical Society (LAFDHS) is an organization dedicated to chronicling and preserving the history and artifacts of the LAFD and to the establishment, operation and maintenance of museums, memorials and educational facilities.

During the last five years the LAFDHS has been successful in establishing two museums, one at old Fire Station 27 in Hollywood (opened October 11, 2001) and one at old Fire Station 36 in San Pedro (opened August 5, 2003).

Our Fallen Firefighter Memorial at old 27's is nearing completion as this book is being published. The William Rolland Educational Institute is also currently under development at the same location.

In addition, a rehabilitation program will soon begin on the Ralph J. Scott, Fireboat 2. Not only will the program repair and restore the boat, it will provide a permanent land-based structure in which to house it in San Pedro.

We invite you to become a member of our Historical Society and, if possible, consider becoming a part of our volunteer family.

Greg Gibson, Battalion Chief LAFD

President
Los Angeles Fire Department Historical Society

Early LAFD History

Founded in 1781 under the auspices of the King of Spain, Los Angeles for many years was a small pueblo serving an agricultural community. The earliest buildings, constructed primarily of adobe clay bricks with tile roofs, were extremely practical and resistant to fires. The storage of large quantities of forage and bedding hay, however, created hazardous conditions that sometimes resulted in large fires. In response to these fires, neighbors would rush to assist in saving the property by forming impromptu "volunteer bucket brigades." These brigades, using three gallon leather buckets and assisted by Native American Indians, worked until the fire was extinguished or burnt out. Since no fire bells or alarms existed, a person discovering the fire might shoot a pistol into the air repeatedly, followed by similar action of others until most of the town was alerted. This type of alarm system was common into the 1880's.

In 1850 the Common, or City, Council was authorized to create a Fire Department. No formal action was taken however until 1871 when the Volunteer Fire Department was organized. Prior to this, Los Angeles did not have a firehouse, firefighting equipment or professional firefighters. In November 1869, during a meeting at Buffums Saloon on Main Street, former San Francisco volunteer firemen, young businessmen, and leaders in civic and social affairs created an informal volunteer organization.

The volunteers operated as Engine Company No. 1 and existed from 1871 to 1874. Their firehouse occupied an adobe building on the west side of Spring Street, between First Street and Temple Street next to the old City Hall. Since the City Council had no funds to purchase a steam fire engine it was financed through private donations and fines levied against those who caused fires. These were mostly vagrants, minorities, laborers, and prostitutes. The first steam fire engine, an Amoskeag, was manufactured in New Hampshire and shipped by train to San Francisco. Since a railway connection did not exist between San Francisco and Los Angeles until 1876, the engine was transported by ship along the coast to Wilmington, arriving in October of 1871. When the volunteers demonstrated the new engine for the public they were disappointed at its poor performance and sent it back. The replacement engine did not arrive until June of 1872. This new Amoskeag was much improved and had a capacity of 750 gallons per minute (gpm) at 80 pounds per square inch (psi). The volunteers had no horses so they had to pull their engine to the fires with long ropes. The volunteers also had a hand pulled hose cart and 100 feet of hose.

In 1872 the City Council appointed an Engineer, George McLain, to operate the engine. He was the only paid employee of the volunteer company and earned a salary of $100 per month. Charles E. Miles was elected by the volunteer members as the first Chief Engineer for a one year, unpaid tenure. In 1884 this position became salaried at $125 per month. On April 4, 1874 the volunteer company disbanded after the City Council took no action toward purchasing two horses to pull the engine.

On April 14, 1874 thirty-eight of the original members of Engine Company No.1 formed a new company and took possession of the equipment. They called their new company 38's Engine Company No.1. To pull the engine to fires they used teams of horses from local stables. The first team to arrive at the firehouse during an alarm was the team employed. The following year the City Council agreed to purchase two horses to pull the engine.

In 1884 the Company moved into the Plaza Firehouse, which became the Los Angeles Fire Department station No.1 in 1886. The Plaza Firehouse remained in service until 1897 and was thereafter used as a warehouse, cafe, cheap hotel, gaming hall, and saloon until it reopened as a fire museum in 1960. It currently is part of the state El Pueblo Historical Park and is operated by a group of fire enthusiasts known as the Box 15 Club.

A second volunteer company was organized in May of 1875 as the Confidence Engine Company No. 2. It was on Main Street near First Street and remained at that location until 1887. They operated a horse drawn 900 gpm Amoskeag steamer and a two-wheeled hose reel.

Several hose companies were established in the outlying areas as the city grew. The first, in 1878, was the Park Hose Company No.1, with a horse drawn cart on Spring Street north of Sixth Street near what is now Pershing Square. In 1879 the Vigilance Hook and Ladder No.1 was organized on Main Street near the Plaza. They obtained a horse-drawn Babcock "Village" ladder truck equipped with the new soda-acid hand operated extinguishers. In 1884 East Los Angeles Hose Company No. 2, with a hand pulled pumper, was established on Truman Street near Downey Avenue, vicinity of North Broadway east of the Los Angeles River. That same year Morris Vineyard Hose No.3 was located at 15th Street and Hill Street. They ran with a hand drawn four-wheeled hose reel.

In addition there were some private volunteer outfits operating in the city. The Southern Pacific Railroad started operations in Los Angeles in 1872. They maintained a hose reel and a switcher locomotive equipped with a pump and hose to protect the shops and River Depot located just north of the Plaza in an area later known as the Corn Field Yard. The Gas Company on Aliso Street and Center, and the Spring and Sixth Street Railway Co., both kept quantities of hose but no carts.

The paid Los Angeles Fire Department officially began on February 1, 1886. By the turn of the century the Department consisted of 18 fire stations with 120 firemen and 80 horses.

Chapter 1

Volunteers and the Era of Horses

The Exempt Fireman Certificate issued to David Main, a member of 38's Engine Company No.1, presented in 1879.

A parade of the volunteer fire department celebrating their first anniversary on September 30, 1872. The photograph was taken at Main and Temple Streets, near Billy Buffums Saloon.

We honor the first chief of the volunteer department, Chief Charles E. Miles.
June 1876 to March 1880

We honor the second chief of the volunteer department, Chief Jacob Kuhrts.
March 1880 to April 1883

The interior of the restored Plaza Firehouse after it opened as a museum in 1960. The horse stalls are at the rear and there is a turntable on the floor for turning the apparatus.

Right:
We honor the third chief of the volunteer department, Chief Walter S. Moore.
April 1883 to March 1885

We honor the forth and last chief of the volunteer department, Chief Frank Day.
April 1885 to January 5, 1886 (no photo)

Volunteers and the Era of Horses

We honor the first chief of the Los Angeles Fire Department, Chief Walter S. Moore.
February 1, 1886 to September 26, 1887
February 1, 1891 to January 31, 1893
February 1, 1895 to March 31, 1900

The volunteers of the Morris Vineyard Hose Company No. 3 with their hand pulled four-wheeled hose reel. The company was organized in 1884 and was located at 15th and Hill Streets.

The old Plaza Firehouse was built in 1884 to house the volunteer 38's Engine Company No. 1. The building became Fire Station No. 1 in 1886 when the paid department was founded. It is now a museum in the El Pueblo Historical Park and is occupied by a fire buff organization known as the Box 15 Club.

This Hayes ladder truck was the first practical aerial ladder in America. It was invented by Daniel D. Hayes of San Francisco in 1868. A restored Hayes aerial ladder truck is on display at the LAFD Historical Society Museum in Hollywood.

Confidence Engine Company No. 2 at their second house located at 114 W. Ninth Street in 1888. Here, the members and their dogs proudly pose with their straight frame 1875 Amoskeag engine.

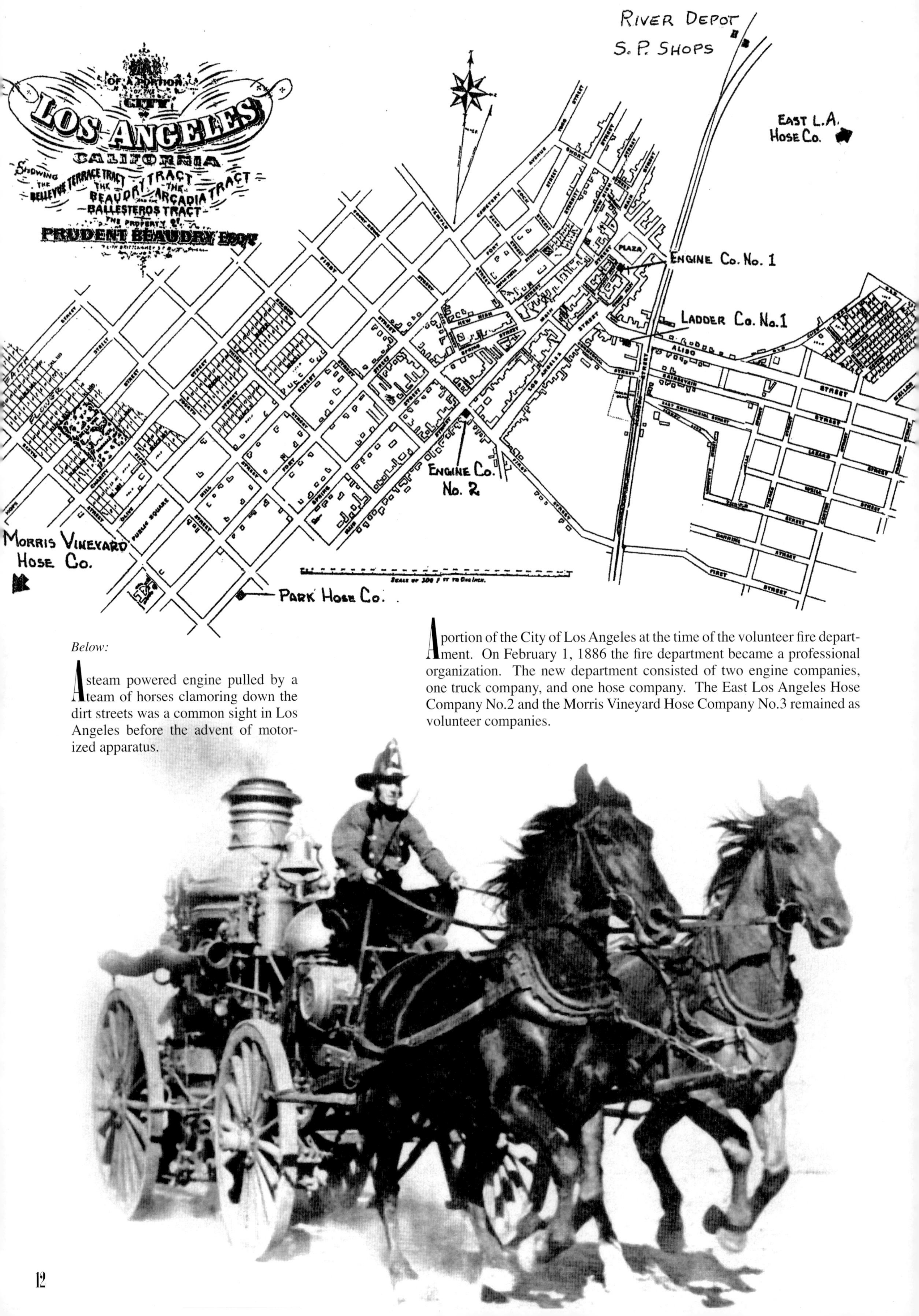

Below:

A steam powered engine pulled by a team of horses clamoring down the dirt streets was a common sight in Los Angeles before the advent of motorized apparatus.

A portion of the City of Los Angeles at the time of the volunteer fire department. On February 1, 1886 the fire department became a professional organization. The new department consisted of two engine companies, one truck company, and one hose company. The East Los Angeles Hose Company No.2 and the Morris Vineyard Hose Company No.3 remained as volunteer companies.

We honor the service of Chief Thomas Strohm.
October 1, 1887 to January 25, 1888
March 22, 1889 to January 31, 1891
April 1, 1900 to February 28, 1905

Firemen with their engine and hose wagon pose in front of new Fire Station No. 2 on East First Street, in the Boyle Heights area, in 1896.

A line-up of horses at the department yards. The powerful geldings were named (l to r) Rusty, Sandy, Buster, Jim, and Blackie. Fire department horses were usually a crossbreed between Morgans and Percherons because of their strength and size. The LAFD retired its last horse in 1921.

We honor the service of Chief Dan A. Moriarty.
January 26, 1888 to February 28, 1889
December 1, 1893 to January 31, 1895

We honor the service of Chief Michael Curran.
February 1, 1893 to November 30, 1893

Horses had a maintenance vehicle too. This wagon carried a forge, horse shoes, and tools to treat the horse's hooves. Here it is in front of Fire Station 5 at 525 East Fourth Street.

A view of the apparatus floor area of Fire Station No. 3. The station was located at 412 North Main Street from 1896 until 1900. The harnesses were designed to drop onto the horses. The alarm panel is at the far right.

Engine Company No. 1 operated this Amoskeag 2nd size, 700 gpm steamer.

Engine Company No. 11 and Truck Company D just after 1900. Ladder trucks were labeled with letters until 1905.

LAFD activity at the Sanborn fire at 530 South Main Street on April 22, 1913.

Left:
Members of Engine Company No. 9 advancing a 2 1/2 inch line into the side doorway of a very smoky building fire.

A horse-drawn aerial ladder truck company responding south on Hill Street near Fifth Street. Note the lack of uniforms on the crew.

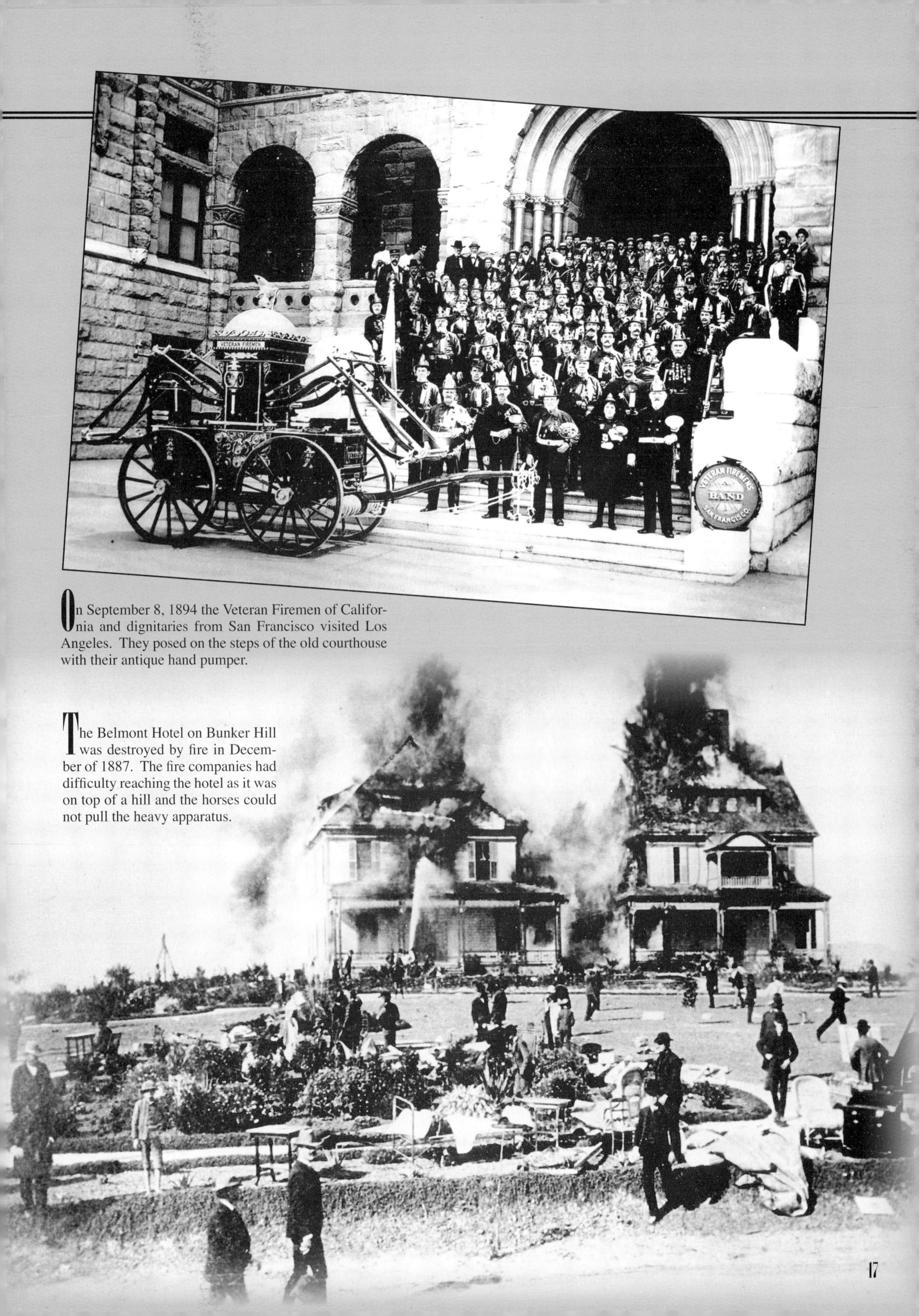

On September 8, 1894 the Veteran Firemen of California and dignitaries from San Francisco visited Los Angeles. They posed on the steps of the old courthouse with their antique hand pumper.

The Belmont Hotel on Bunker Hill was destroyed by fire in December of 1887. The fire companies had difficulty reaching the hotel as it was on top of a hill and the horses could not pull the heavy apparatus.

Fire Station No. 18 and its chemical hose wagon. The station opened at 2616 South Hobart Boulevard in 1906 and closed in 1968. The vines are rapidly covering the building.

We honor the service of Chief Walter Lips.
March 1, 1905 to May 23, 1910

Hose Company No. 2 was located on West Winfield Place from 1900 to 1916 and from 1920 to 1924.

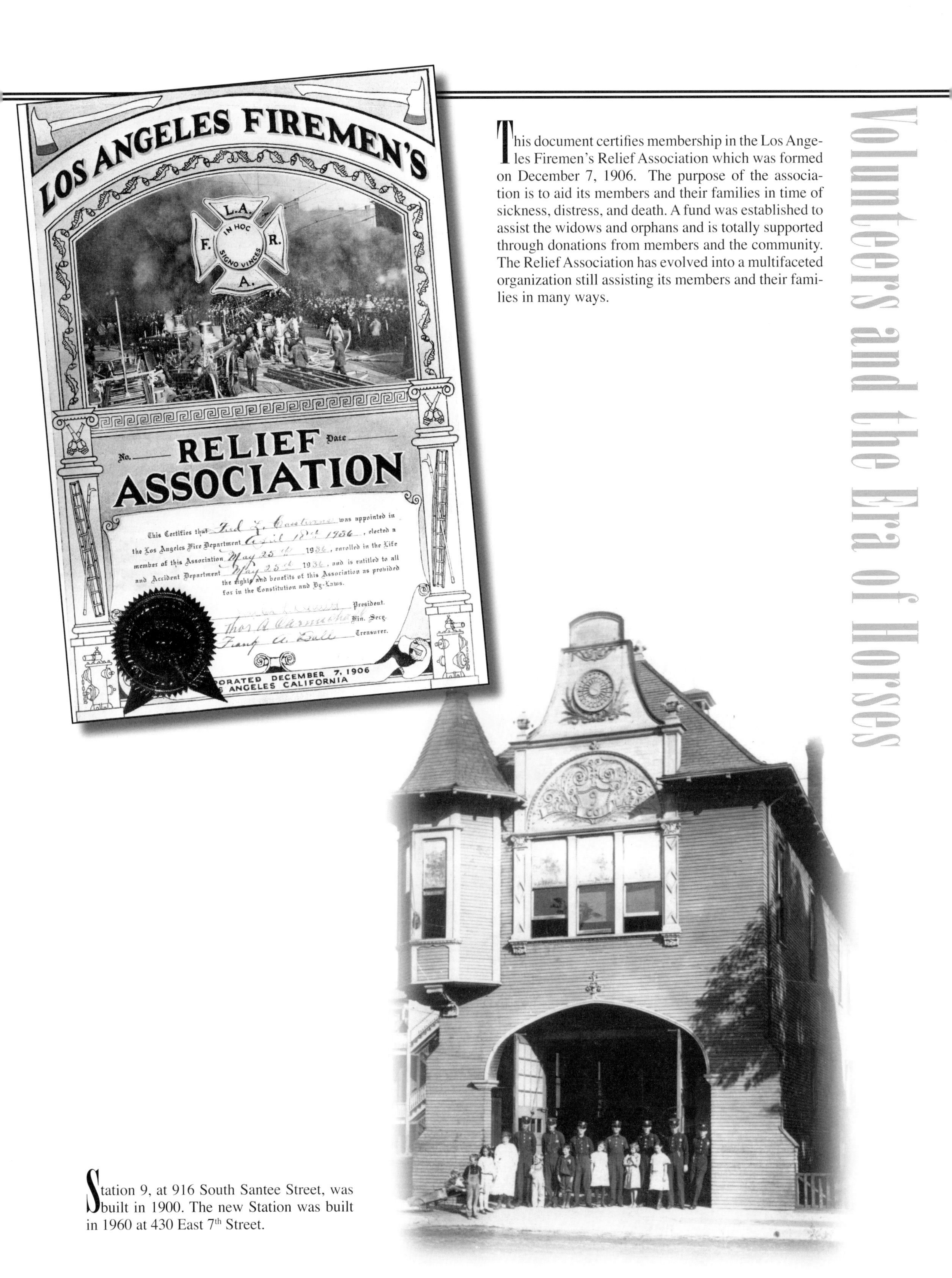

LOS ANGELES FIREMEN'S

No. ______ RELIEF ASSOCIATION Date ______

This Certifies that ______ was appointed in the Los Angeles Fire Department ______, elected a member of this Association May 25th 1936, enrolled in the Life and Accident Department May 25th 1936, and is entitled to all the rights and benefits of this Association as provided for in the Constitution and By-Laws.

______ President.
______ Fin. Secy.
______ Treasurer.

...ORATED DECEMBER 7, 1906
...S ANGELES CALIFORNIA

This document certifies membership in the Los Angeles Firemen's Relief Association which was formed on December 7, 1906. The purpose of the association is to aid its members and their families in time of sickness, distress, and death. A fund was established to assist the widows and orphans and is totally supported through donations from members and the community. The Relief Association has evolved into a multifaceted organization still assisting its members and their families in many ways.

Station 9, at 916 South Santee Street, was built in 1900. The new Station was built in 1960 at 430 East 7th Street.

LAFD firemen testing the new 1905 Gorter Water Tower in 1906.

The fire at the Los Angeles Pacific Railway office in 1908 attracted a large group of onlookers. The Gorter Water Tower is at work in the center of the picture.

Wagon and Engine 19 exercise their gallant steeds near their station at 1435 North Main Street in 1908.

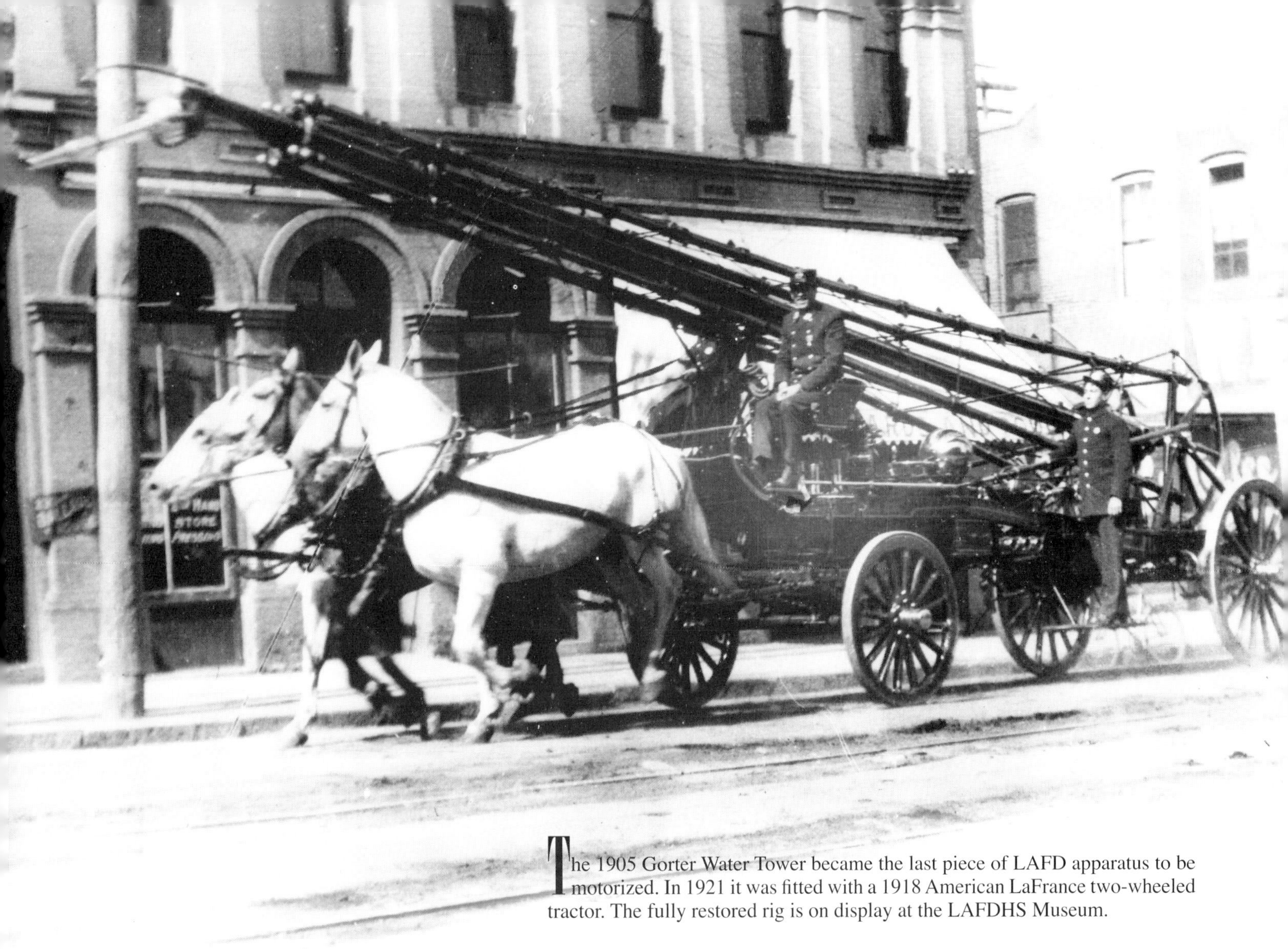

The 1905 Gorter Water Tower became the last piece of LAFD apparatus to be motorized. In 1921 it was fitted with a 1918 American LaFrance two-wheeled tractor. The fully restored rig is on display at the LAFDHS Museum.

The captain and crew of Engine 17 take a break after loading hose onto their chemical hose wagon in 1910.

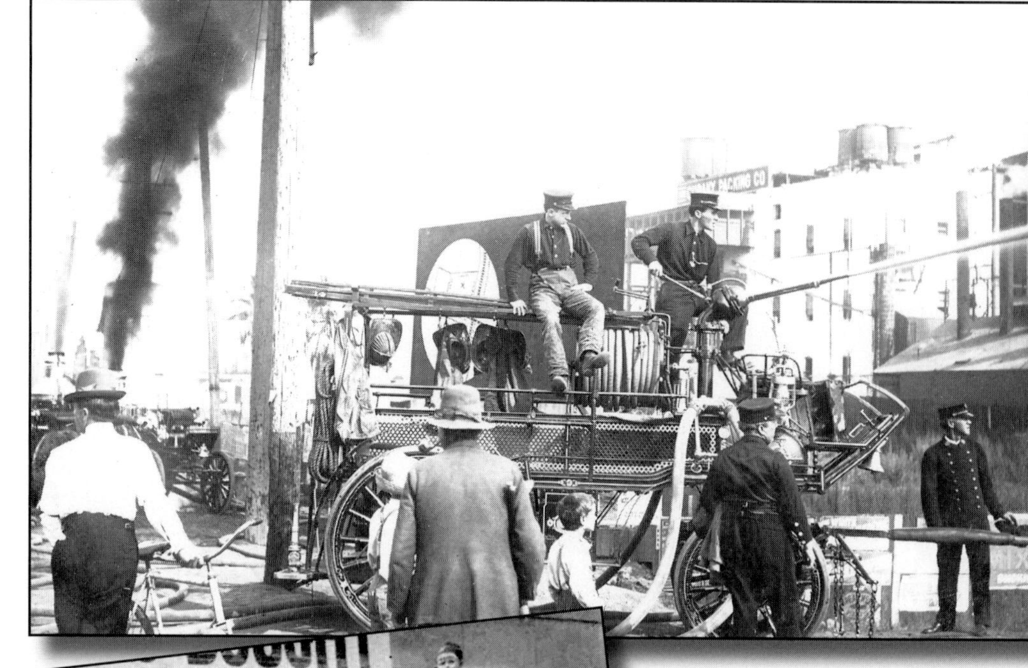

The hose wagon with the engine company uses a monitor to direct a heavy stream.

Engine Company No. 18 decorated for the Los Angeles Fiesta parade in 1908. The LAFD was always a willing participant in community functions, showing civic pride in their service to the neighborhood.

A police officer keeps a wary eye on the photographer taking a picture of the destruction left by the bombing of and fire in the Los Angeles Times building on October 1, 1910.

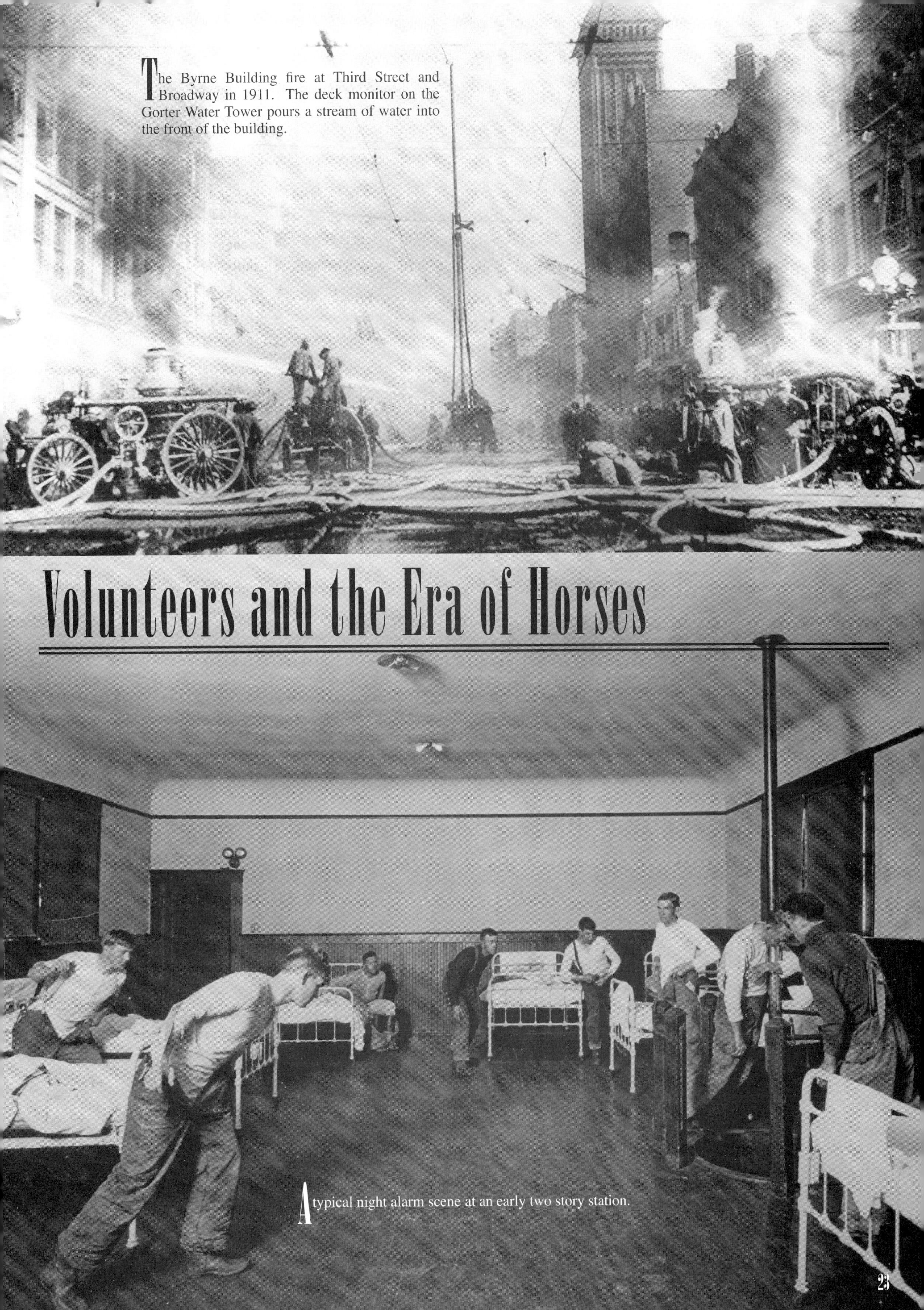

The Byrne Building fire at Third Street and Broadway in 1911. The deck monitor on the Gorter Water Tower pours a stream of water into the front of the building.

Volunteers and the Era of Horses

A typical night alarm scene at an early two story station.

Engine 16's 1904 Nott steamer in action as bystanders continue to monitor the situation. Note the hose wagon in the background.

This circa 1910 photo shows members and mascot of Truck Company No. 1 (formerly truck A) in front of their quarters on Aliso Street. In 1918, this Anderson city service ladder truck was motorized with a 1913 Seagrave tractor. This combination is on display at the museum.

Chief Walter Lips with the 1908 starting line-up of the LAFD baseball team.

Chapter 2

Motorization: The Teens and Twenties

The first motorized vehicle was purchased in 1907. It was an eight passenger Locomobile that was used by the fire commission for inspection trips. The following year a 60 horsepower Haynes roadster was purchased for Chief Walter Lips. Although the Department received a 1908 Tourist chemical hose wagon when the City of Hollywood was annexed in 1910, the first fire fighting vehicle purchased was a 1911 Robinson Jumbo 700 gpm pumper. It was assigned to Fire Station 26 on West Washington Blvd. so that it would be centrally located to respond to any location in the city. Unfortunately the Robinson was not that reliable and broke down frequently. Later, in 1911, the first Seagrave engines and a tractor truck were purchased. Six Christie tractors were purchased to power steam engines in 1914 & 1915. Also, a 1918 American LaFrance two-wheeled tractor was used in 1921 to power the 1905 horse drawn Gorter water tower. This Gorter has been fully restored and is on display at the museum. The last horse was retired in 1921 as the LAFD became fully motorized.

In 1907 the Fire Commission voted to purchase a self propelled Locomobile for their use for inspection trips. It was the first motorized vehicle to serve the LAFD.

The LAFD's first motor driven fire truck was acquired from the City of Hollywood when it was annexed to Los Angeles in 1910. The 1908 Tourist hose truck became Hose Company 7 and was housed in a converted church. The LAFD had to hire the Hollywood Fire Department driver since no one in the department could operate a motor truck. When it rained, the dirt streets of Los Angeles became mud. Note the chains on the rear wheels.

The second motorized vehicle purchased by the LAFD was a 1908 Haynes roadster. The driver was Harry Claiborne whose first job was to drive the chief. At Fire Station 3 the Haynes chief's car was the first vehicle to replace a horse. By 1921 all the horses had been replaced by motorized apparatus.

We honor the service of Chief Archibald J. Eley.
May 24, 1910 to July 17, 1919

Motorization: The Teens and Twenties

A major Downtown fire in the early teens. Note the horse-drawn Gorter Water Tower in use and the unusual 1911 Seagrave aerial ladder truck.

Chief Eley is seen here participating in the Shriners Parade in his decorated Haynes. Note the operating water fountain on the rear of his car.

The first pumping engine purchased by the LAFD was a 1911 Robinson Jumbo seen here in front of its quarters at Fire Station 26. The 700 gpm engine was plagued with mechanical problems and was sold after only ten years of service.

Here is a combination 1911 Seagrave tractor and horse-drawn city service ladder truck. The location is behind Station 23 on Winston Street.

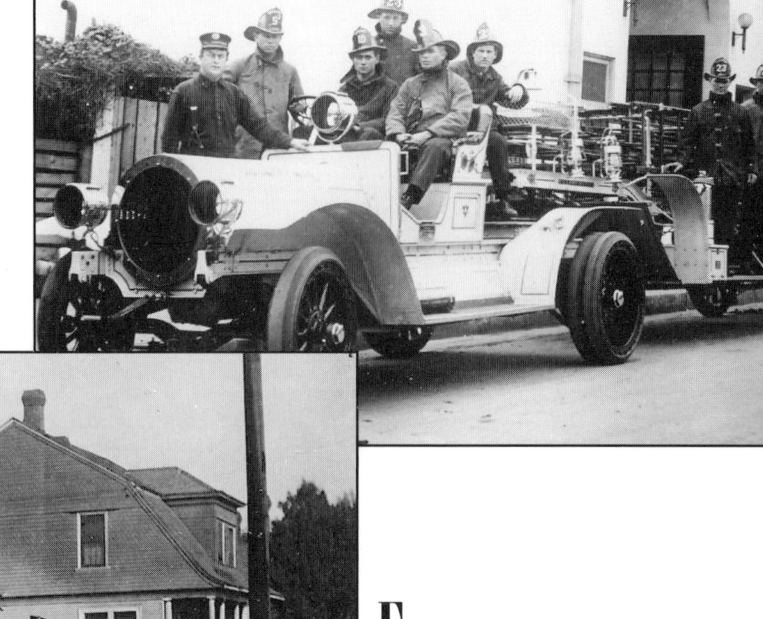

Engine Company No. 30 on South Central Avenue in 1913. A 1913 Seagrave tractor is used to pull the 1904 Nott 700 gpm 2nd size steamer. Fire Station 30 is now the home of the African American Firefighters' Museum.

Chief Eley encouraged women to become volunteer firefighters to assist the LAFD in the residential areas while their husbands were at work downtown. The women volunteers were able to control several fires using hand drawn hose reels. Note the apparent large fire in the background.

In the early years of motorized equipment many combinations were used to utilize the existing horse-drawn apparatus. This is a 1911 Gramm chassis with a horse drawn hose wagon body. With a 40 gallon soda-acid tank, it was Engine 20's hose wagon. Their station was located at 2144 Sunset Boulevard in the Echo Park area.

Left:

1911 Seagrave chemical hose wagon with a Gorter high pressure monitor and a 60 gallon soda-acid tank. This air-cooled, four cylinder, 53 hp, engine was known as the White Hope. As the LAFD's second motor driven apparatus, it was assigned as Engine 3's wagon at their station at 217 South Hill Street.

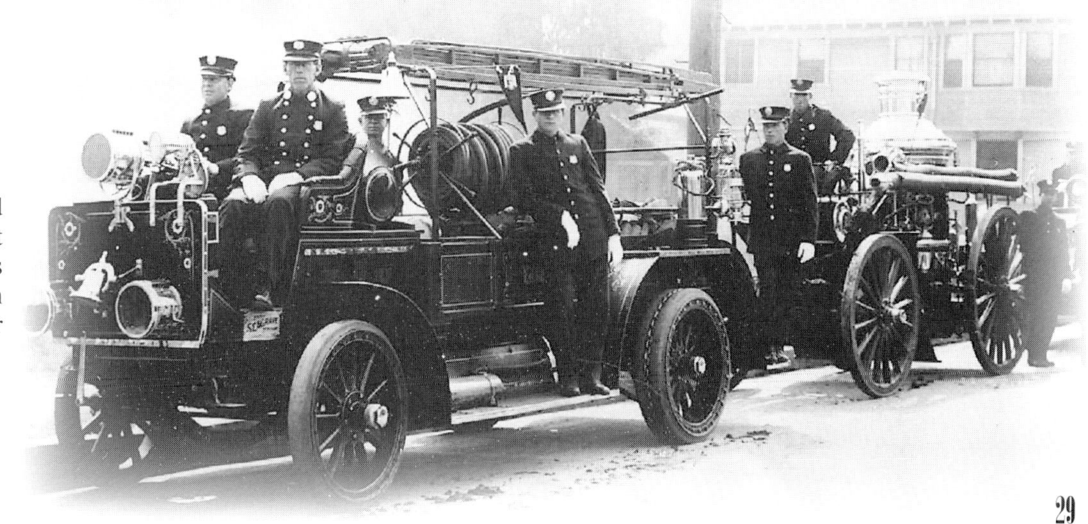

Right:

This 1911 Seagrave buckboard chemical hose wagon was built from a horse-drawn wagon. It was assigned to Engine Company 22 on South Main Street and pulled their steamer.

Posed in front of Fire Station 28 is their 1913 Gorham Seagrave Auto Pumper. It was the first 1000 gpm straight pump purchased by the department.

Below:

A 1914 Christie tractor on an 1899 American LaFrance 2nd size 700 gpm steam powered engine at Fire Station 29 on Western Avenue in 1917.

Men and equipment of old Fire Station 27 at 1625 North Cahuenga Boulevard in Hollywood. The LAFD shared the building with the Police Department on the right. The apparatus on the left is a 1912 Gorham Seagrave Auto Pumper combination hose wagon. Next to it is a 1914 Seagrave city service ladder truck.

Squad No. 1 housed at Fire Station 5 at 525 East 4th Street in 1916. This 1915 Moreland squad truck was equipped with five portable floodlights and a generator.

This 1913 Seagrave tractor is attached to a 1910 Anderson city service ladder truck that contains a 35 gallon soda-acid tank and hose reel. This truck was assigned as Truck No. 1 in 1918 at 1615 South Hill Street. The truck is now on display at the LAFDHS Museum.

The firemen at old Fire Station 27 (1625 North Cahuenga Boulevard) pose with Buster Keaton in front of the station in 1928. Keaton filmed several movies using the station from 1923 to 1928. His studio was located nine blocks south at Cahuenga Boulevard and Eleanor Avenue.

After dinner the crew at old Station 27 in Hollywood gather in their recreation room.

Motorization: The Teens and Twenties

The Los Angeles Fire Department has always depended on the voters of Los Angeles to support ballot measures to maintain fire protection, as seen here in the mid 1920's.

An Early Squad company, wearing protective clothing and gas masks, roll out the back door of old Station 23 in a 1923 Stutz rig.

Firefighters practice their skills at a drill in the 1920's.

A 1914 Byron Jackson basement pump was purchased by the LAFD and was pulled by a standard pumper on a custom built trailer. This unit was housed at Engine Company 16 then located at 139 North Hope Street.

Left:

This 1915 Moreland with a hose body from a Champion horse-drawn chemical wagon had two 60 gallon soda-acid tanks. In 1916 it became Chemical No. 1 at Fire Station 29, located at 158 South Western Avenue.

1915 Morcland chemical hose wagon climbing hills during an acceptance trial. In 1916 it was assigned as Engine 35 at 1314 North Vermont Ave.

This tangle of hoses, or "street spaghetti," was common after a major fire.

This handsome 1923 Seagrave 1000 gpm triple was housed at Fire Station 16 on Hope Street. The headquarters building for the Department of Water and Power now occupies the site.

A 1923 Seagrave tractor trailer spring-operated 85 foot wooden aerial ladder truck with an open tiller. Originally Truck 2, at Engine 4's quarters on Aliso Street in 1923, it moved to Engine 3's quarters the following year.

The crew of Station 57 shows off their 1923 Seagrave triple in1924. The station at 729 West Manchester Boulevard was later relocated to 7800 South Vermont Avenue.

The department shops built four of these foam trucks. A 1924 Moreland truck chassis was used with a large divided tank. One side of the tank carried water-dissolved A solution and the other side carried water-dissolved B solution which, when mixed, produced chemical foam. The trucks contained foam applicators, discharge nozzles, and asbestos suits.

Engine Company 43 with its 1924 REO chemical engine at Fire Station 71 on Bellagio Road in the Santa Monica Mountains In 1925. This station was also used for Mountain Patrol No. 3.

The department bought five of these 1923 Stutz straight frame city service ladder trucks with tillers. They were assigned as Trucks 5, 10, 11, 12, and 13.

A salvage company at work covering property at a fire. In 1923 the LAFD became the first major fire department in the U.S. to operate its own fleet of salvage companies.

This is a copy of the front page of the first Grapevine Magazine which is still the official magazine of the Los Angeles Firemen's Relief Association.

THE GRAPE VINE

A Semi-monthly Magazine for Fire Fighters

VOL. I — LOS ANGELES, CAL., MAY 25, 1925 — NO. 1

BOOST FIRE DEPT. ATHLETICS

OUR BALL TEAM

The formation of one or more baseball teams has been started.

First Assistant Chief J. G. Johnson and Second Assistant Chief F. O. Edwards are at the active head of baseball. They want every man that likes to play and can play ball to send in his name and try out for different positions on the teams. So if you have played ball or think you can play, get in touch with them or call Engine No. 28 and give your name to Barney. We want a fast club to represent the Fire Department, and baseball ability is what players will be judged upon, and not on friendship.

There will be three or four teams formed and then the best players from those teams will be selected for the first teams. We seem to have a scarcity of pitchers, so if you can pitch, don't be backward about saying so.

BARNEY.

* * * * * * * *

Good looking Jack Arnell, the versatile soloist from Engine Company No. 3 was giving the boys an earful the other day about how to get along with the fair sex, he says his motto is to give 'em ... and deny ... ges.

* * * *

"THE GRAPE VINE"

The Grape Vine is being started and will be edited every two weeks, in the interest of athletics and social events amongst members of the Fire Department.

Contributions of interesting items of news will be appreciated and receive every courtesy, if you will mail same to "Barney" Engine Company No. 28.

This will be your paper and your sports. SO Boost.

Nothing is more interesting to the boys of the Department than to know what is going on in the athletic circle, especially the doings of our men.

This paper will be edited by a member, supported by the Department and must be boosted by us all.

What Journalistic talent we lack we will develop.

EDITOR.

THE SPICE OF LIFE

Remarkable Coincidence.—Professor: "Give me a good example of coincidence."

Student: "My father and mother were married on the same day." — Herald and Presbyter.

In Wettest Havana.—Mrs. Calle K. (to inebriated hubby fumbling with the knob to the front door): "What on earth are you trying to do?"

Mr. Calle K.: "S-ssh. Um tryin' t' get Pisshburgh." Times of Cuba

FACTS & FIGURES

How about Baseball?

Do you want a baseball team to represent our Fire Department?

Do you want Hand Ball Tournaments, Smokers, Socials and Dances?

If so, you can have them if everyone will get in and push from the start. We have been challenged by Pasadena, San Diego, and several smaller Fire Departments than our own to play baseball, hand ball and other athletics, and when informed that we didn't even have a baseball team, they expressed surprise that an organization of fifteen hundred men had no athletics or athletic organization of any kind, so let's wake up, fellows, and show them we have a head on our shoulders for something else than to keep our collars from slipping off.

Yours athletically,

BARNEY.

* * * * * * * *

We have a new test for drunks on the fire department now. ... Chief L. H. Davis has a pet snake in a glass jug in his office and if you stay in there for five minutes while he passes him around about you, then ... are sure enough

* * * * * *

Fire crew silhouetted as they battle a blistering fire.

Fire Station 24's 1921 Seagrave hose wagon with red lenses on the headlamps.

Inside a typical single engine bungalow fire station with a 1923 Seagrave engine and crew dressed in coveralls.

Below Right:
This 1926 Seagrave combination hose and chemical wagon with a monitor was assigned to Engine Company No. 28 in Downtown Los Angeles

The crew of new Fire Station 73 in Reseda in 1933 with the 1923 Ford Model "T" chemical hose wagon that was used by the Reseda volunteers before the city provided fire protection to the area.

The first fire station to be built in the San Fernando Valley was this one in Van Nuys in 1919 for Engine 39. The apparatus shown is their 1924 REO grass truck with a 40 gallon tank as it appeared in 1928.

This unusual fire station behind the Eagle Rock Branch City Hall was home to Engine 42 in 1928. Note the hose tower in front.

Engine 5 located at 525 East 4th Street about 1926. Note the motorized 1905 Gorter Water Tower which is now preserved at the LAFDHS Museum.

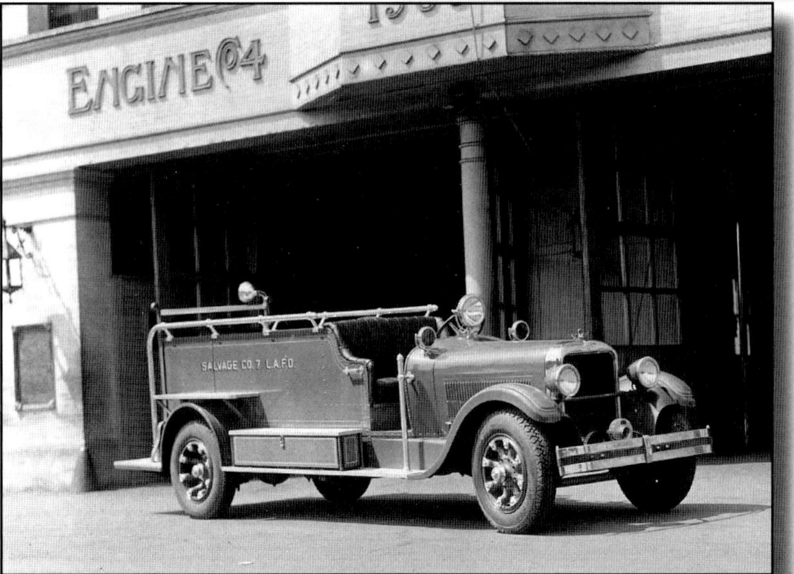

This small salvage wagon, built from a 1928 Studebaker truck, has an open bed for salvage covers. It is powered with a 6 cylinder, 70 hp motor and was used at Fire Station 5 in 1928 and at Fire Station 7 in 1932.

The LAFD shops built this carbon dioxide fire extinguishing system truck from a 1928 Studebaker pickup truck. CO2 Company No. 1 was housed at Fire Station 3 in 1930.

To assist with major brush fires in the hills above Hollywood the department built this hose carrier from a 1925 Mack. It was housed at Fire Station 27.

On March 15, 1929 a fire started in an airplane exhibit at the Los Angeles Motor Car Dealers Association show. Four large tents, covering almost 150,000 sq. feet, burned within 15 minutes. Every vehicle in the show was either destroyed or severely damaged. The loss exceeded one million dollars.

Fire Station No. 14 was built in 1904 for horse-drawn equipment. It is shown here, in 1931, with a 1921 Seagrave 1000 gpm double combination pumper and hose and a 1921 Seagrave chemical hose wagon.

Chapter 3

City Expansion and the Thirties

By the 1930's several of the nearby cities had annexed into the City of Los Angeles. In addition, the suburbs were developing at such a rapid rate that the LAFD could not build and equip fire stations fast enough. To provide fire protection to these areas, volunteer companies were formed for nearly eighty neighborhoods from the harbor to the mountains. The LAFD provided the apparatus for these companies, usually Ford Model "T" chemical hose wagons. The equipment was housed in sheds, barns, and garages and manned by the local residents. A few of these volunteer companies remained in service until the 1950's.

The 1930's were also the period when the department purchased a fleet of streamlined apparatus. In 1937 and 1938 five American LaFrance 400 series triples were bought. These were enclosed crew, or sedan cab, V-12 powered and nicknamed Lulubelles since they were big and clumsy like the cartoon character of the time. Also during that time, four Duplex pumpers, two manifold wagons, two city service ladder trucks, and a 65 foot water tower, all with sedan cabs, were purchased from American LaFrance. Two streamlined Seagrave manifold wagons and an aerial ladder truck were also bought.

Built in 1913, ornate Fire Station 28 served the downtown area until 1969. The old station is now used as a restaurant.

LAFD's only 1938 American La France water tower in action at a greater alarm fire in downtown Los Angeles.

LAFD FIRE STATION 27

1355 No. Cahuenga Blvd.
Hollywood, California

Built in 1930, it was completed after occupancy began on July 1, 1930. Cost of construction was $101,627.

This was the largest fire station west of the Mississippi, with 28 firefighters on duty with 12 pieces of apparatus. This included an Assistant Chief, (division headquarters) and Battalion Chief (battalion headquarters).

Apparatus Lineup:
Assistant chiefs' Buick, and Battalion chiefs' Buick.
Truck Co. No. 9: 1923 Seagrave 85' Aerial, SN 92.
Special Hose Carrier (for brush fires): 1925 Mack, SN 18.
Engine Co. No. 27: 1926 Seagrave Chemical Hose Wagon, SN 70 &
1929 American LaFrance Pump, SN 30
Salvage Co. No. 4: 1929 American LaFrance, SN 845.
Hose Co. No. 2: 1925 Stutz Chemical Hose, SN 179.
2nd Special Hose Carrier: 1930 White, SN 822.
Rescue Co. No. 2: 1930 Studebaker, SN 96.
Not Shown: 1930 Moreland Tank Wagon, SN 60, and 1930 WhiteTransport, SN 138.

The second home for Engine 27 was built in 1930. The new station in Hollywood housed twelve pieces of apparatus and was the largest fire station west of the Mississippi River at that time.

We honor the service of Chief Ralph J. Scott.
July 18, 1919 to April 1, 1940

Before the LAFD had stations in remote, sparsely populated areas, volunteer companies were formed. This volunteer station in Reseda, in the San Fernando Valley, housed a 1923 Ford Model "T" chemical hose wagon supplied by the department.

One of the last volunteer companies in Los Angeles was this group in Playa Del Rey, shown in 1950. The 1928 Chevrolet chemical hose wagon was housed at Charles Market on Culver Blvd.

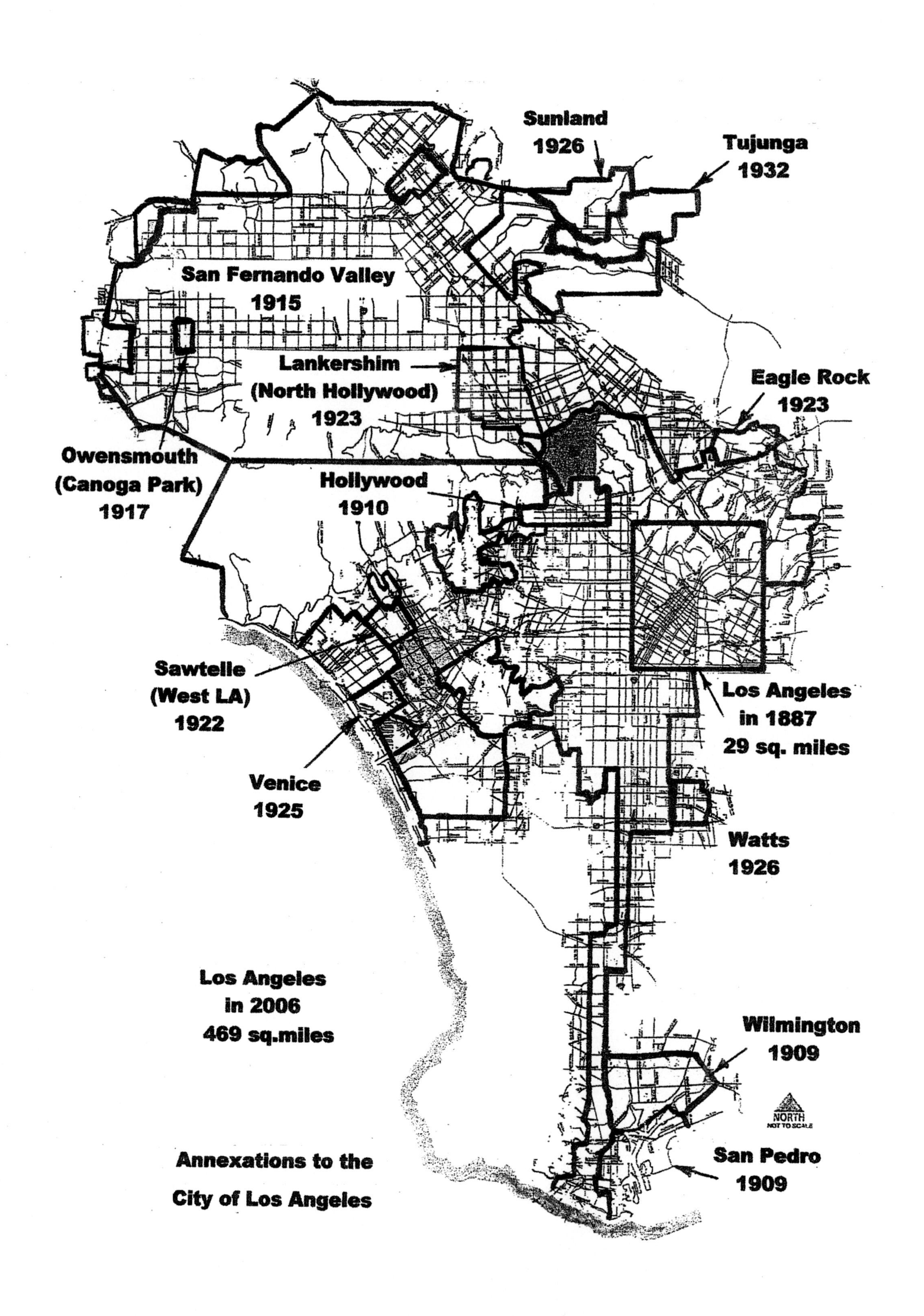
Sunland
1926
Tujunga
1932
San Fernando Valley
1915
Lankershim
(North Hollywood)
1923
Eagle Rock
1923
Owensmouth
(Canoga Park)
1917
Hollywood
1910
Sawtelle
(West LA)
1922
Los Angeles
in 1887
29 sq. miles
Venice
1925
Watts
1926
Los Angeles
in 2006
469 sq.miles
Wilmington
1909
NORTH
NOT TO SCALE
San Pedro
1909
Annexations to the
City of Los Angeles

After the City of Sawtelle was annexed to the City of Los Angeles in 1922 a new fire station was built to house Engine Co. 59. The firemen ran with a 1925 Seagrave triple and a 1922 Ford chemical hose wagon.

San Fernando Valley Area

McKinley Home, Sherman Oaks
Van Nuys
Zelzah (Northridge)
Owensmouth (Canoga Park)
Chatsworth Park
Pacoima
Reseda
Olive Sanitorium
Brandt's Ranch
Girard (Woodland Hills)
Roscoe (Sun Valley)
Ventura Boulevard & Pacoima Boulevard
Week's Poultry Colony (Winnetka)
Laurel Canyon
North Hollywood
Hollywood Country Club (Studio City)
Hauser Heights (Shadow Hills)
Runnymead (Reseda)
Mission Acres
Encino Acres
Sun Valley
Studio City
Sunland
Fernangeles (Sun Valley)
Sepulveda
Sunshine Ranch (Granada Hills)
Tarzana
Granada
Sherman Oaks
Lakeside Park
Canoga Park
Tujunga
Broudt's Road (Warner Center)
Sylmar

Harbor Area

Gardena
San Pedro City Hall
Wilmington Town Hall
National Lumber Yard
San Pedro, two tugboats
San Pedro, Sepulveda & Mesa
San Pedro, 650 W. Pacific
San Pedro, Center near 11th Street
Wilmington, Canal & I Street
Wilmington, Young & End Streets
Terminal Island, Ocean & Caserta
Terminal Island, Ocean & Ontario
Fish Harbor
Los Angeles Ship Building Co.
Harbor City

Westside Area

Palms
Culver City
Westgate
Pacific Palisades
Up Lifters Club, Rustic Canyon
Bel Air
Santa Monica Canyon
Ince Ranch
Beverly Glen
Mines Field, L A Airport
Playa Del Rey
Benedict Canyon

Central City Area

Cottage Home Tract
St. Vincent College Tract
Edendale
Cole Grove
Hollywood
South Hollywood
101 S. Manhattan Place
Cypress Park
Klondike Park
Commonwealth & Middlebury
Rosehill District
Glassell Park
Mount Washington
Atwater Tract
Sierra Vista
Echo Park
Angeles Mesa
Rio Vista
Roger Young Village

Volunteer fire companies from 1910 to 1952 in areas of the city not covered by LAFD stations. The volunteer companies received apparatus, hose and equipment from the city. The apparatus was usually Ford Model "T" chemical hose wagons and housed in small garages and sheds.

The firemen of the City of Wilmington pose on the steps of the Wilmington City Hall on September 19, 1909. The City of Wilmington and its fire department were annexed to the City of Los Angeles that same year

The City of Venice operated with this classic hose truck in 1910 in front of their Fire Station No. 1.

The City of Venice Fire Department, at Station No.1 on Rose Avenue, just prior to annexing to Los Angeles in 1925.

One of the volunteer companies on Terminal Island in 1915. Note the sturdy wooden wall in front of the fire station to protect it and the hand-drawn apparatus from wind blown sand on the low island.

In 1931 the 38 member LAFD band gathered in Exposition Park. The band performed in parades and at other social functions.

City Expansion and the Thirties

Fire Station 31 was built in 1914, re-built in 1929, and closed in 1971. It served the South Los Angeles area from its location at 700 West Slauson Avenue.

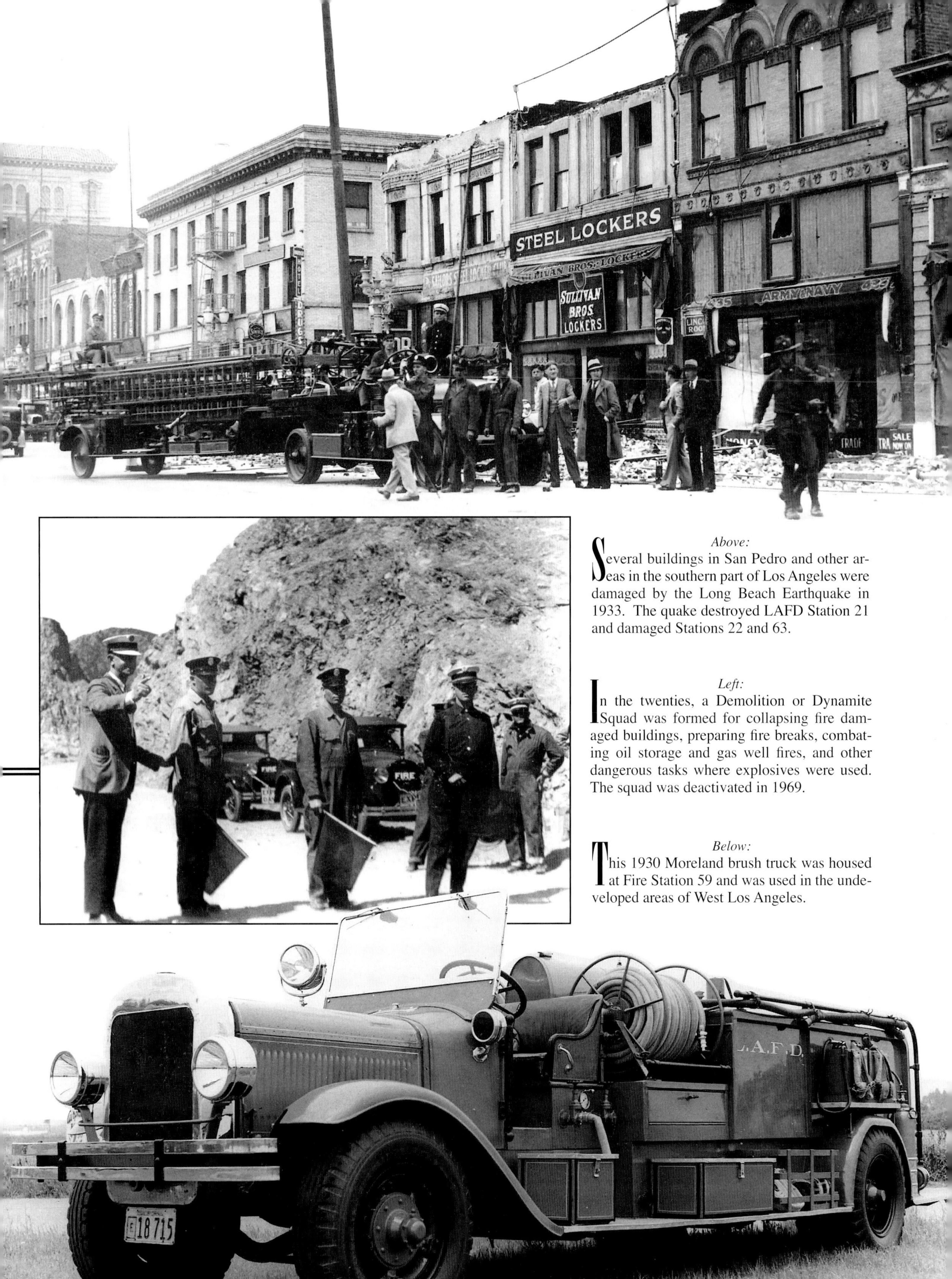

Above:

Several buildings in San Pedro and other areas in the southern part of Los Angeles were damaged by the Long Beach Earthquake in 1933. The quake destroyed LAFD Station 21 and damaged Stations 22 and 63.

Left:

In the twenties, a Demolition or Dynamite Squad was formed for collapsing fire damaged buildings, preparing fire breaks, combating oil storage and gas well fires, and other dangerous tasks where explosives were used. The squad was deactivated in 1969.

Below:

This 1930 Moreland brush truck was housed at Fire Station 59 and was used in the undeveloped areas of West Los Angeles.

Only one of these 1938 American LaFrance water towers was purchased by the LAFD. It was used only once at a fire in the Gray Building on November 6, 1939 and then was put on reserve status. The huge amount of water that the tower put out caused the floors of the burning Gray Building to collapse. Two firemen died of injuries sustained at this fire. The remains of this truck are now owned by the LAFDHS.

Two of these American LaFrance Duplex pumpers were purchased in 1937 and two more in 1938. The concept of Duplexes was conceived by Chief Scott as a means of reducing the numbers of pumpers at major fires. Each one took the place of three conventional pumpers. The Duplexes had two pumps each powered by V-12 engines and had a total capacity of 3000 gpm. These pumpers remained in service until the mid 1960's.

This 1938 American LaFrance manifold wagon ran with and was supplied water by a Duplex pumper.

After their station was destroyed during the Long Beach Earthquake of 1933, Engine Company 21 was moved to a temporary firehouse at 49th Street and Compton Avenue.

Fire Station 41 on North Gardner Street with their 1923 and 1929 American LaFrance apparatus.

Left:
Newly Appointed Fire Chief Ralph J. Scott, receives his badge from Captain Rhoades in 1920.

This 1938 Seagrave 100 foot aerial ladder was the first all steel aerial ladder purchased by the department. It was housed at Fire Station 3 in Downtown Los Angeles.

The Manifold-Duplex system was put to use at this downtown fire at the Gray Building on South Broadway in November of 1939. This was the first and last time these systems and the water tower were used together at a fire.

The Battalion Chief working out of Fire Station 44 in Cypress Park drove this classy 1937 Buick Coupe.

The LAFD bought five of these 400 series American LaFrance triples in 1937 and 1938. They had 1500 gpm pumps and were among the first department apparatus to have enclosed crew cabs. They were nicknamed Lulubelles. This one is at Fire Station 50 in 1939. One of these pumpers is on display at the museum in Hollywood.

The last city service ladder truck purchased was this 1938 American LaFrance. The LAFD had two of these and one of them is now owned by the Historical Society.

The LAFD parks their apparatus behind each other in the stations. Here is the inside of Fire Station 3 with its 1938 Seagrave aerial ladder, 1937 American LaFrance Duplex pumper, 1931 Seagrave salvage wagon, and Buick chief's car. Not shown is the 1938 Seagrave manifold wagon in an adjacent bay.

No one was injured at this spectacular fire at the popular Palomar Ballroom on October 2, 1939 located at 214 South Vermont Avenue.

Chapter 4

The War Years and the Auxiliary

During the Second World War, over 300 of the LAFD's 1700 uniformed members enlisted in the armed forces. This shortage of personnel resulted in the closure of several fire stations. Also, since the threat of enemy air raids could cause widespread fires, the Department Initiated a Civilian Auxiliary. The civilian volunteers were trained by the Department and at first used an assortment of private cars and trucks. These vehicles were stored in various private facilities such as garages, storefronts, and gas stations. During the war, these vehicles were gradually replaced by civil defense fire fighting trucks. By the end of the war, there were over 140 Auxiliary fire companies in service.

Members of Auxiliary Fire Company 47-A proudly pose with their converted fire truck outside Fire Station 47 on September 13, 1942.

Auxiliary companies practicing to keep the Pico-Union area safe from fire in the event of an air attack.

The truck used by Auxiliary Company 68-A in front of Fire Station 68 at 5213 West Pico Boulevard. The auxiliary companies supplemented the LAFD during World War II when large numbers of paid firemen joined the military. Many civilians who were unable to join the military found they could serve their country in other ways. They joined the auxiliaries and helped to protect the city of Los Angeles.

Many businesses donated trucks for the use of the auxiliaries. The Golden State Creamery Co. donated several delivery trucks like this one used by a group of volunteers on South Central Avenue in 1942.

Most of the auxiliary companies operated out of private garages and businesses like No. 64-A in this converted store in the Watts area.

Left:
Members of Auxiliary Company 26-A receiving first aid supplies from the local citizens. The auxiliaries were equipped and trained by the LAFD and received support from neighbors in the community

In 1942 a dozen oil barges, provided by the Sunset Oil Company, were used as temporary fireboats in the harbor. They were equipped with monitors and pumps and towed to fires with tugboats.

The War Years and the Auxiliary

Above:

By the end of the war there were over 140 auxiliary companies in service and over 2000 trained volunteers to man them. Here, six volunteers train under the guidance of a captain in front of Mountain Patrol No. 1 and Engine 76. Notice how loaded down with fire hose that "Woodie" station wagon is.

Above Right:

Firefighters attack a greater alarm fire near Downtown Los Angeles.

Right

Multiple hand lines in use at a major lumber yard fire.

Below:

A mass wet drill at Westlake Park (renamed MacArthur Park after the war) using trailer mounted pumps. By 1944 the number of volunteers diminished as the threat of an air attack declined.

Chapter 5

Post War Boom: Into the Fifties

During World War II, very few new apparatus were purchased by the LAFD. With the end of the war, Los Angeles grew rapidly and, although the Department began replacing old equipment, they still operated some vehicles from the 1920's and 1930's well into the 1950's and early 1960's. During this period, eighteen 1945 Pirsch triples; twenty 1948 Mack triples, hose wagons, and salvage squads; nine Yankee/GMC salvage squad; fifteen Seagrave triples; and two Seagrave 85 foot aerials were added to the fleet.

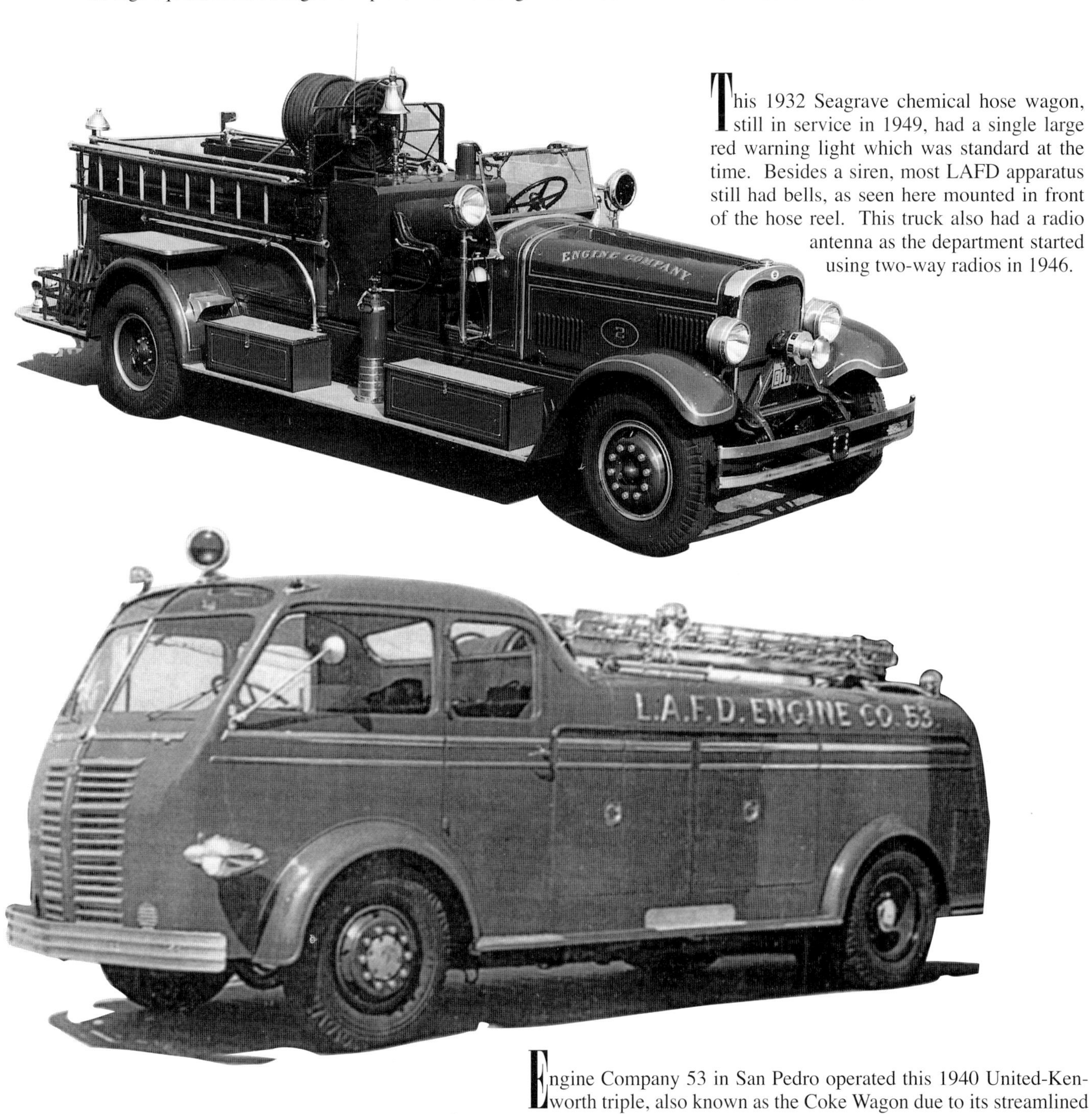

This 1932 Seagrave chemical hose wagon, still in service in 1949, had a single large red warning light which was standard at the time. Besides a siren, most LAFD apparatus still had bells, as seen here mounted in front of the hose reel. This truck also had a radio antenna as the department started using two-way radios in 1946.

Engine Company 53 in San Pedro operated this 1940 United-Kenworth triple, also known as the Coke Wagon due to its streamlined delivery truck appearance. Two of these rigs were purchased by the department and served until 1957 when they were sold to Mexico.

Street cars were a common sight in Los Angeles until 1961 when the last one was replaced with gasoline powered buses. The hose bridge was a solution of an old problem to allow street cars to pass over hose lines at a fire.

We honor the service of Chief John H. Alderson.
May 20, 1940 to December 29, 1955

A new 1929 American LaFrance pumper was assigned to Fire Station 1. It was front line equipment when this picture was taken in 1948. The LAFD still used red lanterns on the rear of their apparatus.

A silent night at old Fire Station 13. But the silence will soon be broken by the sound of the alarm bell or by the clatter of the Los Angeles Railway street car passing by. The station was located on Pico Boulevard at Kenmore Avenue from 1904 until 1950. The wooden spire from the hose tower is on display at the LAFDHS Museum.

Below:

This 1948 Mack squad at Fire Station 23 on East Fifth Street, was used for the transportation of additional man power. The entire crew had breathing apparatus and distinctive green shields on their helmets. They were nick-named the Green Hornets. The old station was built in 1910 and was used until 1960.

To protect the high value area of Downtown Los Angeles, this 1948 Mack fully manned salvage wagon was stationed at Fire Station 28. Shown here outside of Fire Station 16 it carried lights, mops, sawdust, smoke ejectors, and salvage covers.

Left:
Engine 3 in 1947 consisted of this 1938 Seagrave manifold wagon and a Duplex pump. The manifold, seen here at a fire at 4th and Bunker Hill Streets, carried 2000 feet of 3 1/2 inch hose in back and an additional 1500 feet of 2 1/2 inch hose in the transverse compartments. The fireboat-sized monitor could take up to a 3 inch tip.

On February 20, 1947 a tremendous explosion of overheated, unstable chemicals completely destroyed the O'Connor Electroplating Company on Pico Boulevard. Fifteen people were killed and over 150 injured, with more than 50 other structures damaged in a 300 foot radius of the plant.

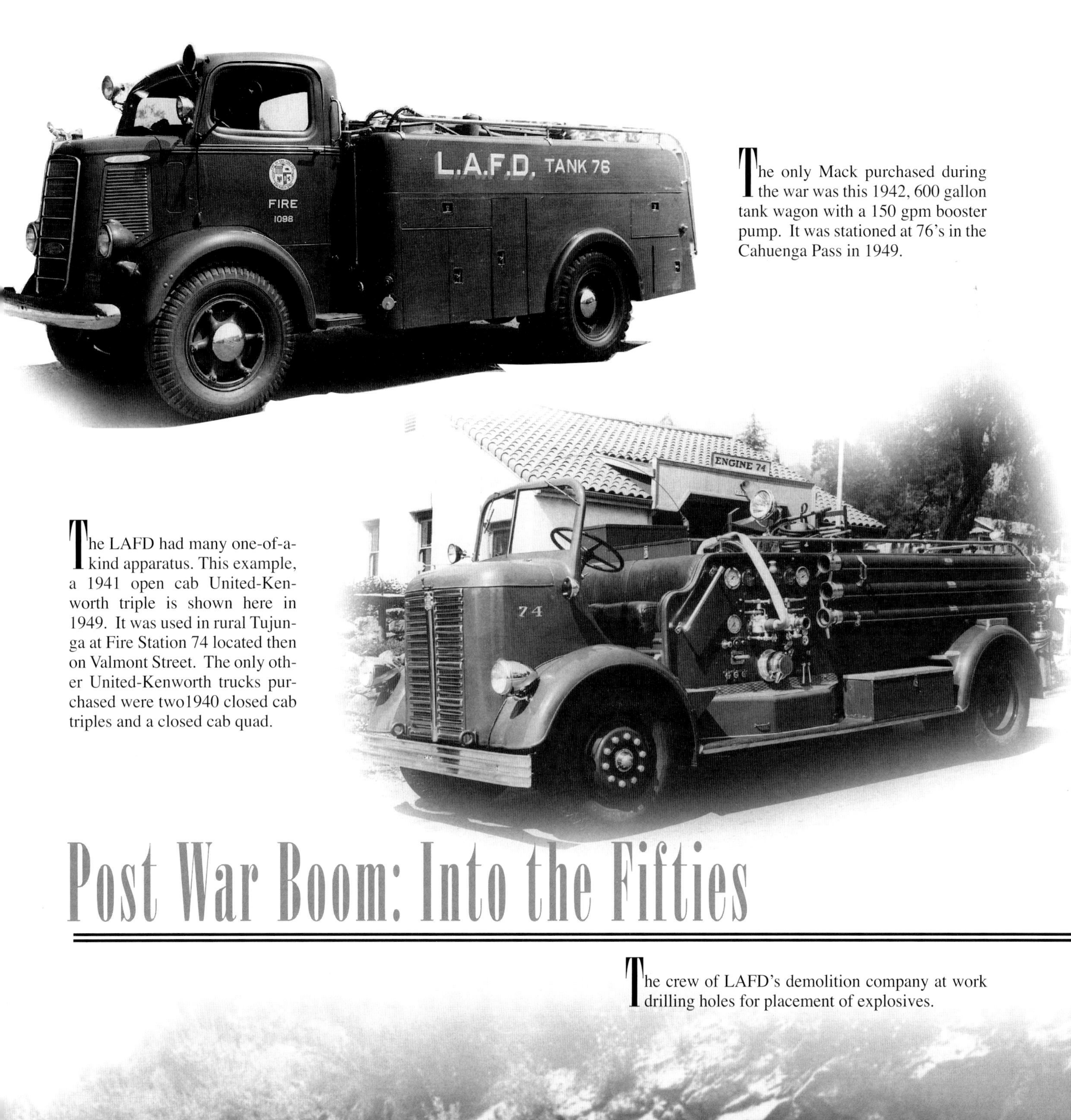

The only Mack purchased during the war was this 1942, 600 gallon tank wagon with a 150 gpm booster pump. It was stationed at 76's in the Cahuenga Pass in 1949.

The LAFD had many one-of-a-kind apparatus. This example, a 1941 open cab United-Kenworth triple is shown here in 1949. It was used in rural Tujunga at Fire Station 74 located then on Valmont Street. The only other United-Kenworth trucks purchased were two1940 closed cab triples and a closed cab quad.

Post War Boom: Into the Fifties

The crew of LAFD's demolition company at work drilling holes for placement of explosives.

Here is a display of the various tools and equipment a 1931 Seagrave salvage wagon carried in 1945. Since the department no longer has salvage wagons similar salvage materials are now carried on the truck companies.

The LAFD tried to get the most out of its apparatus purchases. Here is a 1918 Seagrave triple still in use as Engine 80 in 1944. This apparatus still had a right hand drive and overhead ladder racks. Note the firemen riding on the tailboard. The department stopped allowing this practice in the1980's.

Above:

This command and communications unit was used at major incidents to assist with radio communications.

A firefighter from Engine 35 runs through a smoky greater alarm fire on Sunset Boulevard in 1958. Firefighters now wear gloves as part of their protective clothing.

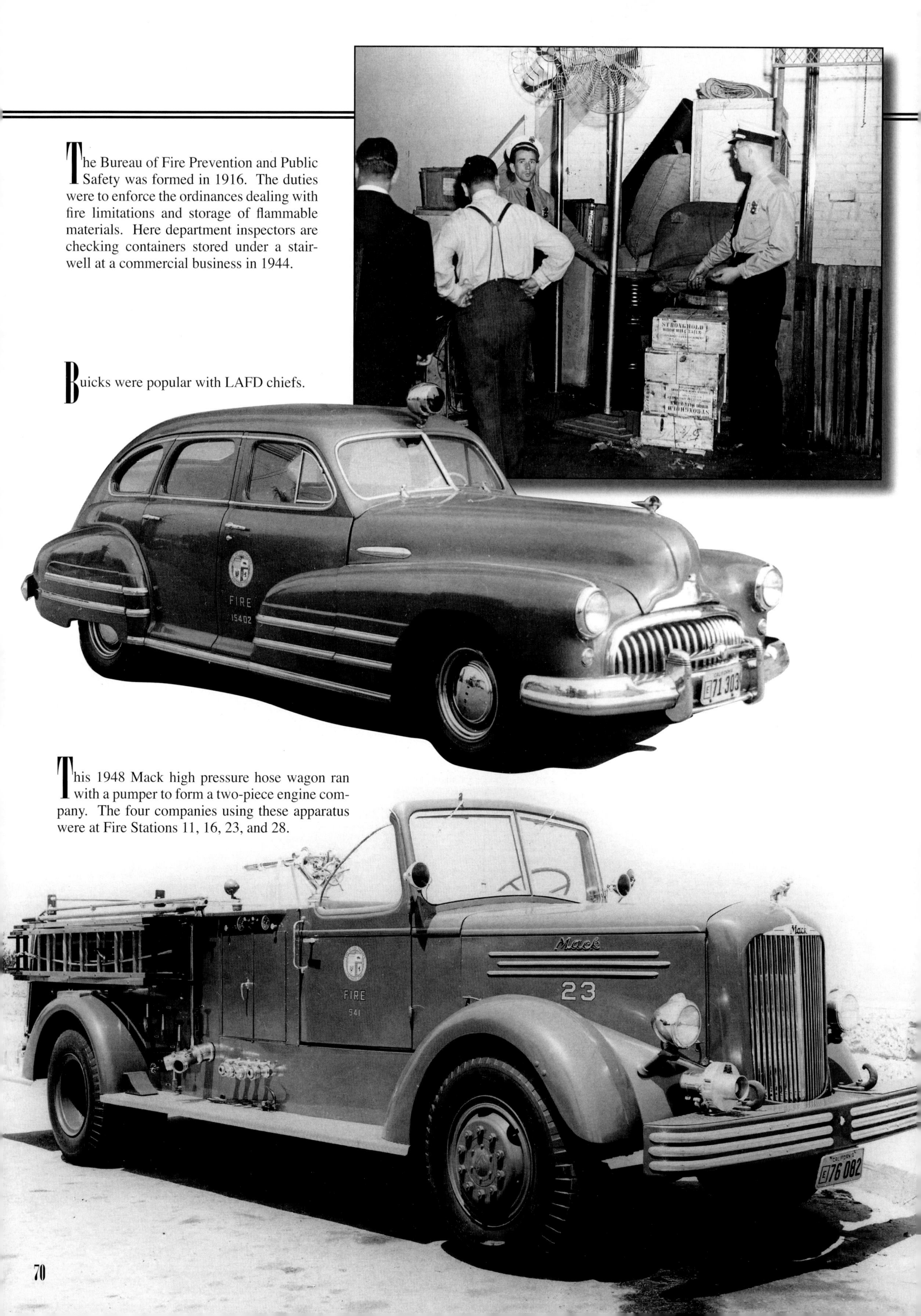

The Bureau of Fire Prevention and Public Safety was formed in 1916. The duties were to enforce the ordinances dealing with fire limitations and storage of flammable materials. Here department inspectors are checking containers stored under a stairwell at a commercial business in 1944.

Buicks were popular with LAFD chiefs.

This 1948 Mack high pressure hose wagon ran with a pumper to form a two-piece engine company. The four companies using these apparatus were at Fire Stations 11, 16, 23, and 28.

Three engines like this one were purchased in 1943 and were so popular with the department that four more were ordered in 1945. This 1945 Kenworth triple was assigned to Fire Station 78 in the Studio City area of the Valley.

When the 101 Hollywood Freeway was built near Downtown Los Angeles in 1949, Fire Station 6 at 1279 West Temple Street was in its path. Here we see the station on blocks, being moved a block north to a new site at 534 East Edgeware Road. While the building was being moved, the apparatus was temporarily housed in the abandoned gas station in the foreground.

Three people were rescued from the third floor of this rooming house at 411 South Bixel Street on February 11, 1949.

Above:
Another odd piece of equipment is this 1951 Seagrave combination assigned to Fire Station 40 and designated Engine 86. The truck has a pump, ladders, and hose, but no water tank. Note the high hose bed. This was certainly a rig for tall firemen.

Right:
The Demolition squad was assisted by this compressor unit on a 1942 Ford truck.

Post War Boom: Into the Fifties

This unusual 1949 Mack manifold wagon featured a four door cab with dual windshields. The Mack replaced a 1938 Seagrave manifold at Station 3.

The horses pulling antique Engine 1 get a water break during a special tour through Downtown in the early 1950's promoting a fire protection ballot measure.

When old and new apparatus were stationed together a nice contrast resulted, as shown here at Fire Station 27. This station is now the location of the LAFD Historical Society Museum and Memorial in Hollywood.

Members of Fire Station 17 in front with their apparatus around 1949. Shown are a 1949 Buick chief's car, a 1928 American LaFrance Duplex pumper, and a 1928 Seagrave manifold wagon. Fire Station 17 is located in an industrial area near Downtown.

Chapter 6

The First Century In Color

LAFD seal

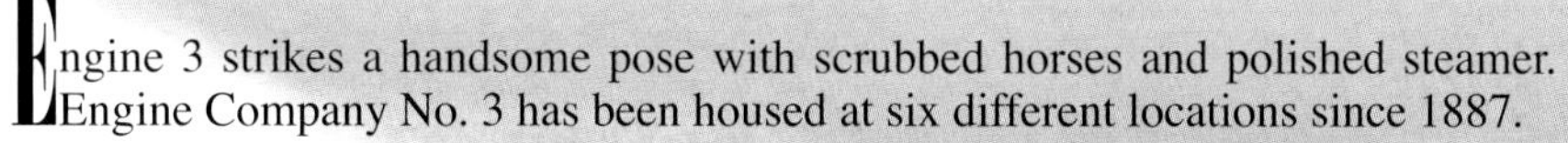

Engine 3 strikes a handsome pose with scrubbed horses and polished steamer. Engine Company No. 3 has been housed at six different locations since 1887.

Below:
1923 Seagrave wooden 85 foot aerial ladder truck with an open tiller.

Engine Company No. 68's 1945 Kenworth triple with unusual rear windshield. Fire Station 68 at 5213 West Pico Boulevard was built in 1929.

The Palms area, in the western part of Los Angeles, was protected with this 1940 United-Kenworth triple at Station 43 on National Boulevard.

Ornate Spanish architecture was used on Fire Station 56 located on Rowena Avenue in the Silverlake area. The station was built in 1924 and was in use until 1989. It also now serves as a restaurant.

Two of these Crown Firecoach engines, with 2000 gpm pumps, were purchased in 1963.

Only two of these 1938 American LaFrance sedan cab city service ladder trucks were purchased by the department. They were the last city service, or non aerial, ladder trucks to be ordered by LAFD.

This 1949 Seagrave triple operating out of Fire Station 33 was one of fifteen purchased from Seagrave after World War II.

Left:
The LAFD celebrates the arrival of new Fire Boat 4 in 1962.

Below:
Every young child dreams of becoming a firefighter..

The First Century In Color

One of the first apparatus to protect the Van Nuys Airport was this 1944 International dry powder crash truck.

When a fallen firefighter is put to rest, hundreds of fellow firefighters come to pay their respects and bid him or her farewell.

This 1938 American LaFrance Duplex pumper was in service at Fire Station 27 in Hollywood. It is seen here at a drill in the Hollywood Bowl parking lot on a Sunday morning in 1960.

This 1942 Mack tank wagon had a 600 gallon water tank and a 150 gpm pump. It was assigned to Mountain Patrol No.1 on Mulholland Drive.

Engine Company 25 was built in 1911 at 2927 Stephenson Ave (Whittier Boulevard). Engine 25 was relocated to Los Angeles County Engine 2's old quarters. In 1979, Engine 25 moved into its new quarters back at 2927 Whittier Boulevard.

Right:
Fire Station 9, built in 1899 and in service until 1960, with a 1938 Seagrave manifold wagon in the doorway. The manifold wagon ran with a 1938 American LaFrance Duplex pumper.

Below:
Arson investigators were assisted by this special mobile unit mounted on a F600 Ford truck.

Fire Station 62 at 3631 Centinela Avenue was opened in 1950 in the Mar Vista area. It replaced an old station on Rose Avenue in Venice that was acquired with the annexation of the City of Venice in 1925. The present station is due to be replaced in 2007.

Firefighters engaged in cutting holes in the roof in a well involved fire at an apartment house to ventilate the fire.

Fireboats 3 and 4 fighting a scrap metal fire on a ship. This type of fire has occurred on several occasions due to spontaneous combustion from cutting oils.

Below:

Three men died in the fire at the Dome Hotel at Second Street and Grand Avenue in the Bunker Hill area. The hotel was fully involved when the first firefighters arrived on the scene on July 25, 1964.

The First Century In Color

Fireboat 2, the Ralph J. Scott, bores into the wharf fire at Berth 232 on June 13, 1977. A favorable wind temporarily carries the deadly creosote filled smoke away from the crew.

Aftermath of the explosion of Liberian tanker M. V. Sansinena at Berth 48 on December 17, 1976. Note that the blast blew the ship sideways about 80 feet from the dock and part of the ship's structure landed behind the dock. Nine people died and many more were rescued by the crews of Fireboat 3 and 5.

Fireboat 4 hammers a stubborn wharf fire with a sweep from its stern at Berth 232 as clouds of smoke billow from the burning timbers.

Wooden aerial ladders like this one on a 1923 Seagrave were commonly used by LAFD until 1938. Some even extended into the 1950's on reserve apparatus.

Before Los Angeles was concerned about air pollution the city used to burn the accumulation of excess vegetation on vacant lots. The LAFD maintained a fleet of these 1953 GMC booster tanks, shown here at the old shops in 1959, to protect exposed adjacent property.

In 1962 the LAFD purchased seven of these GMC tank wagons. This one responded out of station 99, which opened in 1963, on Mulholland Drive in the Santa Monica Mountains brush area.

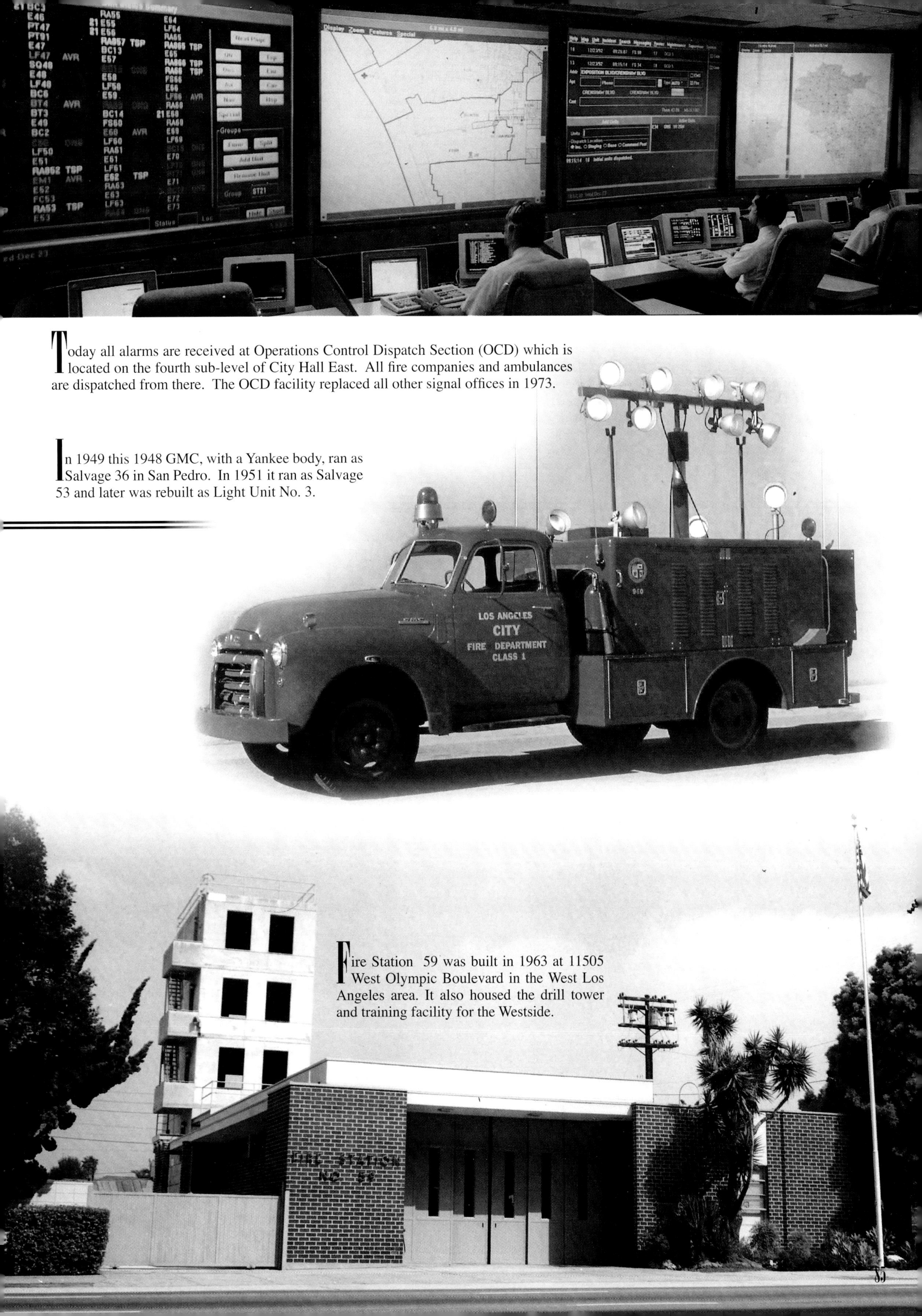

Today all alarms are received at Operations Control Dispatch Section (OCD) which is located on the fourth sub-level of City Hall East. All fire companies and ambulances are dispatched from there. The OCD facility replaced all other signal offices in 1973.

In 1949 this 1948 GMC, with a Yankee body, ran as Salvage 36 in San Pedro. In 1951 it ran as Salvage 53 and later was rebuilt as Light Unit No. 3.

Fire Station 59 was built in 1963 at 11505 West Olympic Boulevard in the West Los Angeles area. It also housed the drill tower and training facility for the Westside.

On March 1, 1978 this Continental Airlines DC-10, bound for Honolulu, blew two tires on takeoff causing it to swerve off the runway. 10,000 gallons of fuel from a ruptured wing tank were ignited by the sparking wheel rims as passengers began evacuation. It took only six minutes for the crew from Crash 80 to extinguish the flames and the death toll was limited to three passengers.

During the Northridge Earthquake on January 17, 1994, a large water trunk line and a high pressure natural gas line ruptured. The resulting fire burned five houses on Balboa Boulevard in Granada Hills. Fortunately, no deaths or serious injuries occurred.

The members of Fire Station 33 and Truck 95 pose with their apparatus in front of the Los Angeles Memorial Coliseum in honor of the 1984 Olympics which were hosted by the City of Los Angeles.

Opposite Page:

The GATX fire in San Pedro, August 8, 1972, lights up the night sky.

This U.S. Air Boeing 737 passenger jet collided, while landing, with a smaller commuter plane that was waiting on the runway at LAX on February 1, 1991. The planes skidded into a vacant fire station. The crash resulted in the deaths of all twelve on the smaller plane and 22 on the U.S. Air jet.

On March 28, 1971 LAFD firefighters responded to a fire at Monty's Restaurant on the 21st floor of a Westwood high-rise. It took fire crews 30 minutes to knock down the flames.

The 6.7 Northridge Earthquake jolted the City of Los Angeles early on the morning of Martin Luther King Day in 1994. This three story, 120 unit apartment building at 9565 Reseda Boulevard, in Northridge, collapsed and crushed the first floor. These cars were crushed to within three feet of the ground. 18 residents were killed in the building collapse.

This helicopter tender is a converted 1957 Ford pick-up. It carried aviation gasoline, jet fuel, a portable fuel pump, litter basket, water tank and other supplies to service the helicopters.

In 1958 the LAFD purchased five of these Mack triples. Like this one at Fire Station 58, they were used as pumpers since they lacked transverse hose beds.

Civilians gave what help they could to assist Los Angeles firemen during the 1965 Watts riots as they fought fires on both sides of the street in this South Los Angeles neighborhood on a hot August day

Los Angeles City and County firefighters were pushed to their limits while being shot at and bombarded with rocks and bottles while they attempted to put out hundreds of arson fires during the Watts riots.

Late in the day the acting Governor of California called in the National Guard to control the looting and arson. The police, sheriffs deputies, and Guard troops did their best to protect the firemen while they moved from fire to fire.

Above:
Engine 82, a 1964 Seagrave, on patrol in the Hollywood Hills.

Right:
1972 Crown triple with a 50 foot telescoping Squrt. The LAFD owned one telescoping Squrt and one articulating Squrt.

Below:
The aftermath of the Continental Airlines crash at LAX.

One of three 1968 Bell jet-powered helicopters hovers over one of the department's first helicopters, a 1962 Bell 47-63B, at Van Nuys Airport. By 2006 the LAFD had a fleet of six jet-powered helicopters.

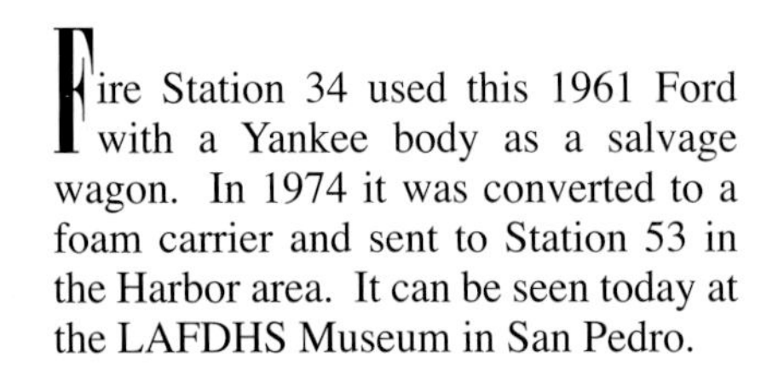

Fire Station 34 used this 1961 Ford with a Yankee body as a salvage wagon. In 1974 it was converted to a foam carrier and sent to Station 53 in the Harbor area. It can be seen today at the LAFDHS Museum in San Pedro.

This 1967 Yankee GMC, which began service as a salvage wagon, was one of two purchased by LAFD. In 1980 it was converted to a hazardous material squad and assigned to Fire Station 4.

Many special apparatus were built at the department shops like this 1948 Mack that was converted from a salvage wagon to a helicopter tender. This rig was assigned to the LAFD Air Operation section at the Van Nuys Airport.

This 1955 Yankee Oshkosh tanker is shown at Mountain Patrol No. 1 in the spring of 1960. It was one of two such rigs assigned to the mountain brush areas.

A 1968 Kenworth tractor and trailer hauling a Caterpillar DG bulldozer. It was designated as Transport No. 1 Mountain Patrol and was also used for hauling portable water tanks and road graders.

This 1953 GMC one ton truck is typical of the patrol rigs used by the Mountain Patrol. It carries a 90 gallon water tank and 300 feet of one inch hose.

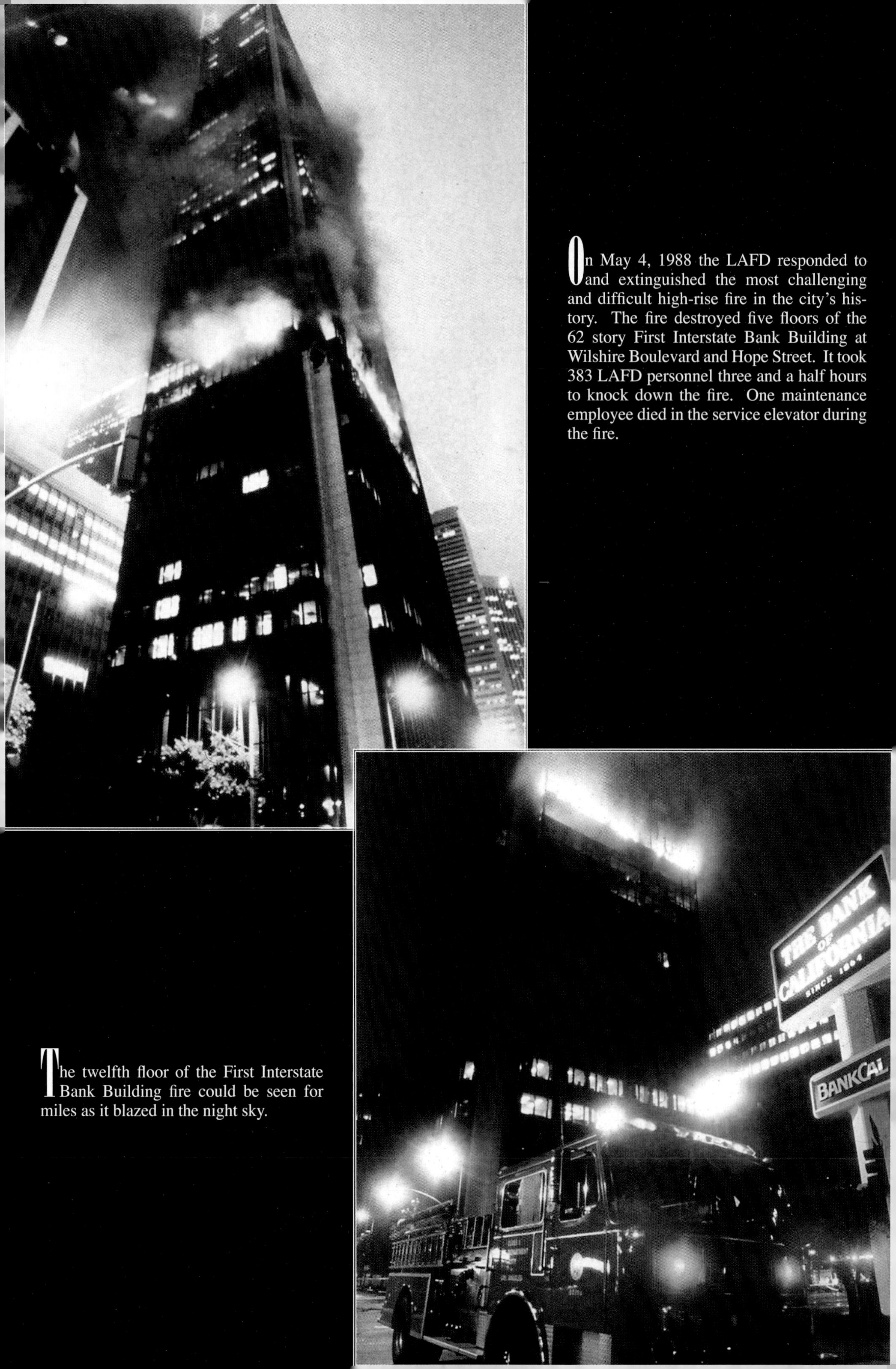

On May 4, 1988 the LAFD responded to and extinguished the most challenging and difficult high-rise fire in the city's history. The fire destroyed five floors of the 62 story First Interstate Bank Building at Wilshire Boulevard and Hope Street. It took 383 LAFD personnel three and a half hours to knock down the fire. One maintenance employee died in the service elevator during the fire.

The twelfth floor of the First Interstate Bank Building fire could be seen for miles as it blazed in the night sky.

The "Maid of the Mists," Fireboat 2, hurls water high into the air during one of its water displays. These displays were common to welcome first time visits of new ships to the harbor.

Fireboat 2, the Ralph J. Scott, in quarters at Fire Station 112 in 1990.

Fireboat 2, the Ralph J. Scott, slips out of its cavernous boathouse at Berth 227 on Terminal Island. The vessel was quartered there from 1926 until 1986 and was the LAFD's most powerful apparatus.

Firefighters search through the debris of a collapsed building at the Veteran's Hospital in Sylmar after the earthquake in 1971.

Three of these 1968 Walter-Yankee crash trucks were in service at Los Angeles International Airport (LAX).

To extend the working life of this 1938 Seagrave 100 foot aerial ladder, this 1943 Kenworth tractor was attached in 1963.

This 1964 Walter-Yankee-FWD crash truck served the Van Nuys Airport.

This 1969 Crown 50 foot Snorkel was assigned to Heavy Task Force 11 in the Downtown district.

Above:

1974 Mack wrecker with a Holmes #850 crane at Fire Station 27 in Hollywood. LAFD's heavy utility companies, now called heavy rescues, are used to assist in rescue operations.

Below:

On September 27, 1980 firefighter Frank Hotchkin, from Truck Company No.1, died from injuries sustained after falling through the fire weakened roof at the Naval and Marine Corps Reserve Center in Elysian Park. The building on Stadium Way is now home to LAFD's training center and is named for the fallen firefighter.

This 1959 FWD high pressure hose wagon was equipped with two booster pumps and ran as part of a two-piece engine company. Shown here responding to a second alarm, it was assigned to Station 83 in Encino.

When Van Nuys Airport received a new crash truck, this 1961 Yankee-FWD foam truck was put on reserve status.

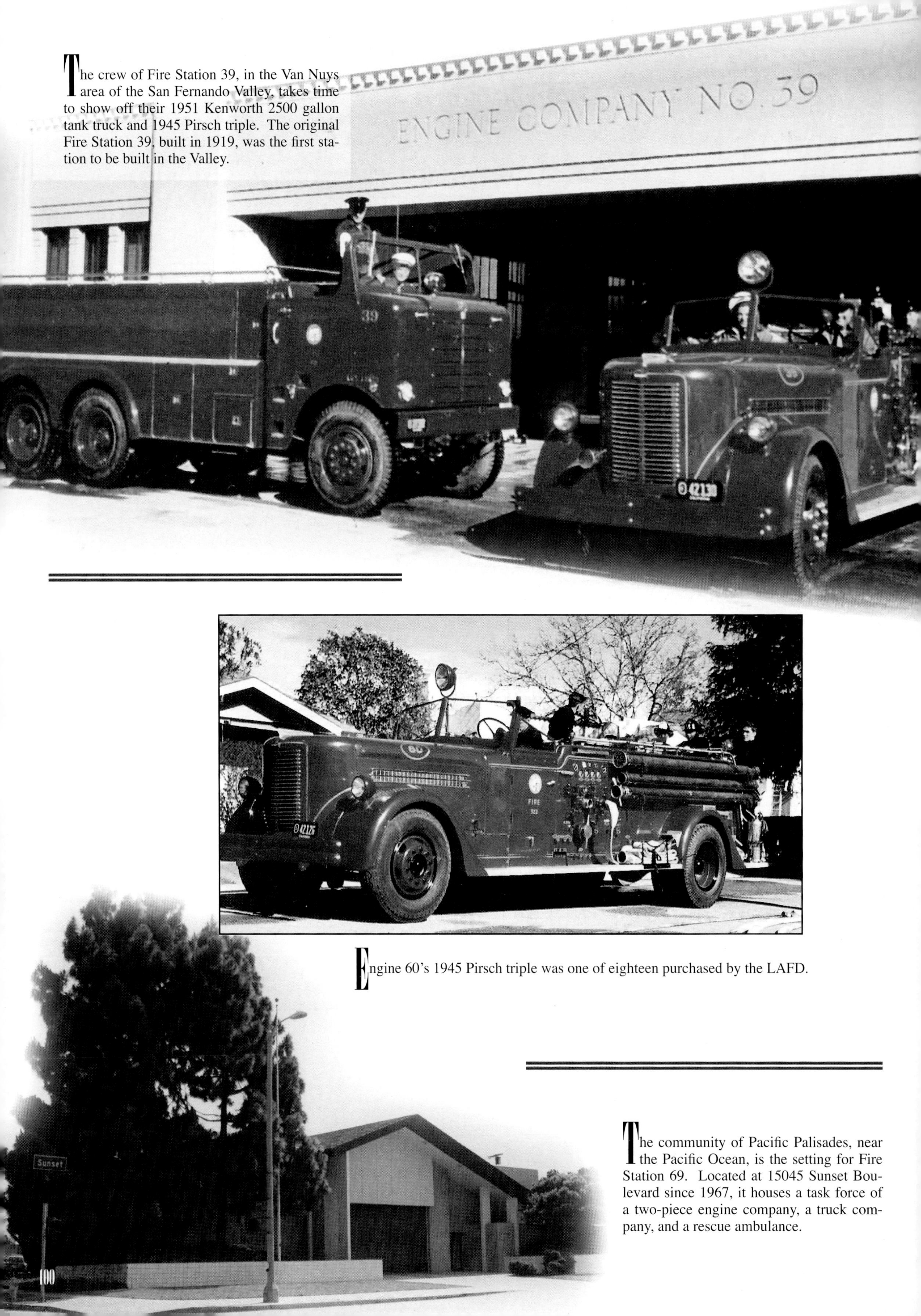

The crew of Fire Station 39, in the Van Nuys area of the San Fernando Valley, takes time to show off their 1951 Kenworth 2500 gallon tank truck and 1945 Pirsch triple. The original Fire Station 39, built in 1919, was the first station to be built in the Valley.

Engine 60's 1945 Pirsch triple was one of eighteen purchased by the LAFD.

The community of Pacific Palisades, near the Pacific Ocean, is the setting for Fire Station 69. Located at 15045 Sunset Boulevard since 1967, it houses a task force of a two-piece engine company, a truck company, and a rescue ambulance.

Fire Station 39 in Van Nuys was the home of this 1948 Mack high pressure hose wagon.

Task force operations were adopted during the Watts riots in 1965. The heavy duty task force consisted of a single engine company, a two-piece engine company, and a truck company. LAFD had heavy duty task forces at Fire Stations 3, 9, 11, 15 and 27. The heavy duty task force at 15's later moved to Fire Station 61.

The fire at the Proud Bird Restaurant at 11022 South Aviation Boulevard, near LAX, in December 1984. This arson fire resulted in the death of one firefighter during a flashover. The Medal of Valor was awarded to a fellow firefighter who tried to rescue him after he became trapped in the building.

The crews and apparatus of Crash 80 on the taxiway at LAX in 1974.

The First Century In Color

The streets around the Central Library were completely blocked by apparatus during this extremely difficult fire on April 29, 1986. Sixty companies of Los Angeles firefighters were involved in suppressing this fire.

Rescue Ambulance 13 used a Ford E350 with a Southern body and sported the two-tone color scheme.

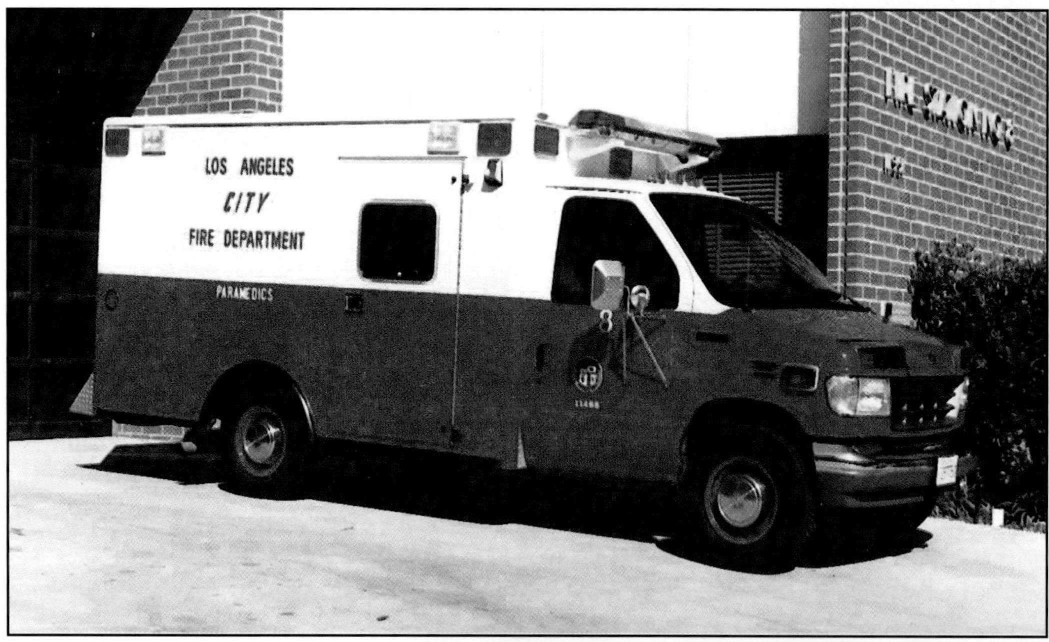

The LAFD upgraded their fleet of ambulances with these larger modular types. Shown is a 1993 Ford assigned to Fire Station 8.

This 1996 Seagrave triple assigned to Fire station 51 at LAX is the only LAFD engine painted chrome yellow as required by FAA regulations.

This firefighter from Engine 33 stays low and directs his water stream directly into the inferno.

Fireboats 2, 3, 4, and 5 participate in a drill. By 2006 Boats 2, 3, and 5 had been replaced with new boats, as well as Boat 1 (not pictured).

In the evening of April 25, 1979 a firefighter was killed while battling this fire at the Mullin Lumber Co. at 7151 Lankershim Boulevard in North Hollywood. The firefighter was killed when the aerial's ladder-pipe came loose and knocked him to the ground. The fire was later found to have been set by burglars after they failed to open the safe.

The crew of Engine 10 ducks and runs for cover as the wall of a building falls toward them. This fire, at a variety store on West Pico Boulevard in 1984, took 21 companies of firefighters and two ambulances to bring under control.

Known as a Suspended Maneuvering System, or flying fire engine, this firefighting platform could be suspended by a cable 500 to 1000 feet below a heavy lift helicopter. It contains a 210 horsepower propulsion engine and four thrust nozzles to move it into position. Unfortunately, the device was never used by the department and was put in storage.

Chapter 7

The Crown Era: The Sixties, Seventies, and Eighties

In 1953 the LAFD began purchasing Crown Firecoach apparatus manufactured by the Crown Coach Co. of Los Angeles. Between 1953 and 1974, the department purchased at least 135 pieces of Crown apparatus. Included in the Crown fleet were two 75 foot aerials, two 50 foot Squrts, four 50 foot Snorkels, two 85 foot Snorkels, 18 high pressure hose wagons, a heavy rescue truck, and a tractor transporter. The Crowns were the first LAFD apparatus to have flat front open cabs with crew seats at the rear of the cab. After the Watts riots of 1965 the Department began installing roofs on their open cab units. Although the Crown Coach Co. stopped building fire apparatus in 1981 the Department's Crowns saw service into the 21st century.

Dalmatian dogs were a common sight with fire apparatus for many years. Duke the fire dog watches over the parked engine. One theory is in the horse-drawn era, the Dalmatians helped calm the horses.

44 companies of firefighters fought this greater alarm fire at an apartment house at 1609 North Normandie Avenue which resulted in the death of three tenants.

We honor the service of Chief William L. Miller.
January 17, 1956 to July 16, 1965

In 1959 the three story condemned and abandoned Robert Louis Stevenson Junior High School building on South Indiana Avenue was set on fire as a test to determine what would happen to a school in the event of an unintentional fire. The purpose was to help prevent loss of life in classrooms in other schools. It also gave the LAFD practice in fighting this type of fire.

We honor the service of Chief Raymond M. Hill.
April 25, 1966 to May 31, 1975

We honor the service of Chief Kenneth R. Long.
June 1, 1975 to June 29, 1977

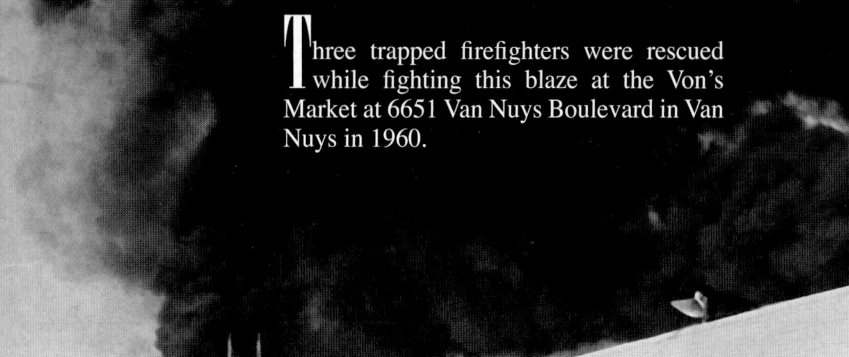

Three trapped firefighters were rescued while fighting this blaze at the Von's Market at 6651 Van Nuys Boulevard in Van Nuys in 1960.

At 5:31 AM on September 13, 1970 dispatchers at the Westlake Signal Office received a call of a fire at the Ponet Square Hotel at 1249 South Grand Avenue. The Ponet fire was the worst apartment hotel fire in Los Angeles to that time. Firefighters rescued 80 people from the flames, but 19 lost their lives. Many victims jumped to their deaths to escape the smoke and fire. The fire spread rapidly due to the open stairways and corridors. On November 17, 1971 the City Council passed an ordinance that required all buildings more than two stories in height to have enclosed stairways and self closing doors which are now known as Ponet doors.

On August 8, 1972 a 36 foot tall tank containing gallons of jet fuel exploded during a fire at the GATX Corporation in San Pedro and the tank shot into the sky like a rocket. Fireboat 2 supplied water from the harbor for the hose lines. The fire was finally extinguished when Crash 80's foam truck from LAX was used to pump foam onto the fire.

Members of a truck company prepare to open the roof to ventilate a fire at a residence in the Hollywood Hills in 1970.

Above:
These three young women are helping to promote the importance of fire safety during fire prevention week in 1960. They are shown inside Fire Station 27 in Hollywood.

Below:
Engine companies fought a losing battle trying to protect homes with wood shingle roofs during the Bel Air fire of 1961.

Thick fog caused this Flying Tiger Lockheed Super Constellation to crash just east of Fire Station 89 on Laurel Canyon Boulevard in the San Fernando Valley. The recruit training class in the drill tower responded to the incident. The crash, in 1962, killed eight people including the two aboard the cargo plane.

This 1963 Crown manifold wagon was a super combination triple that replaced the 1938 LaFrance manifold wagon which was in service for 25 years. The Crown is on display at the Historical Society Museum.

This was the path of destruction through a Baldwin Hills neighborhood after the failure of the Baldwin Hills Reservoir dam on December 4, 1963. When the dam collapsed millions of gallons of water rushed down through the homes with little or no warning. Cloverdale Avenue became a raging river of water, mud, and debris. Firefighters rescued 2000 people from the floodwaters and three helicopter pilots earned Medals of Valor for rescuing 18 victims from balconies, roofs, and windows. As a result of the helicopter's performance a second helicopter was approved for purchase. The dam failure resulted in the loss of 8 lives, 123 dwellings, 670 apartment units.

The Central Library in Los Angeles was built in 1926 and, because of its construction and design, the fire, which began on April 29, 1986, is said to have been the most difficult to have ever been fought. It took 60 companies of firefighters seven and a half hours to control the fire. 50 firefighters were injured fighting the fire in the narrow corridors of the library.

During the evening hours of January 28, 1966 a fire occurred on the tenth floor of the Commercial Exchange Building at the corner of Eighth and Olive Streets. Arriving firefighters could not access the water supply from the standpipes due to a faulty installation of the piston type inlets.

We honor the service of Chief John C. Gerard.
June 30, 1977 to June 6, 1982

Los Angeles High School at 4600 West Olympic Boulevard caught fire as it was being demolished in 1971. Truck 61, a 1960 Pirsch 100 foot aerial, and Engine 61 are shown among the firefighting force that took three hours to control the stubborn blaze.

This 1968 Crown 85 foot Snorkel elevated platform truck was the first apparatus of its size to be purchased by the department. At a fire at 710 South Broadway on July 5, 1970 the truck fell over onto its right side while the platform was being raised. One firefighter was fatally injured and two others suffered injuries. As a result the apparatus was never used again.

In 1976 six structures were destroyed, six people died, and 24 were injured in the explosion and resulting fire when an underground gasoline pipeline was ruptured by a construction company bulldozer. Firefighters were confronted with thousands of gallons of burning gasoline at the fire on Venice Boulevard and Bagley Street in the Palms area.

Above:

Four Crown 50 foot Snorkels were delivered to the LAFD between 1969 and 1971. Engine Co. 3's Snorkel is shown at a spectacular fire at 129 West College Street in 1979.

Right:

National Guard troops, with rifles in hand, ride along on Truck 64 during the Watts riots in 1965.

Two firefighters were seriously injured and one firefighter from Truck 60 was killed at this fire on January 28, 1981 at Cugee's Restaurant at 5300 Lankershim Boulevard in North Hollywood. The firefighter was killed when he fell through the roof of the burning building. After a long investigation it was determined that the fire was intentionally set. Three people were found guilty of arson and sent to prison.

The 32 story Occidental Tower fire at 12th and Olive Streets in 1976 was one of the early modern high-rise fires in Los Angeles. The fire on the 20th floor took over 300 firefighters to control and resulted in the creation of the Incident Command System (ICS) which was soon adopted by fire departments all over the world.

This incendiary fire at the O.B. Saloon on Melrose Avenue in March of 1979 was brought under control by eight companies of LAFD firefighters.

Background photo:
On August 8, 1984, 55,000 gallons of petroleum products fed this greater alarm fire at the Bortz Oil Co. warehouse on North Spring Street. 34 firefighters were treated for chemical burns caused by the flammable materials floating on the water runoff.

An out of order alarm box can be disastrous when a fire occurs.

Below:

Firefighters from Engine 83 and Engine 90 are seen here using hand lines to knock down this fire at the front door of the Toys R Us store in Van Nuys in 1979.

Above:

It took 14 companies of firefighters to control this fire on North Sycamore Avenue in Hollywood.

Rising from the smoke, the captain of Engine 55 watches over the fire fighting operations.

Chapter 8
Mountain Patrol

The City of Los Angeles contains over 170 sq. miles of brush in the Santa Monica Mountains from Griffith Park to Topanga Canyon, in the Santa Susana Mountains north of the San Fernando Valley, and in the San Gabriel and Verdugo Mountains northeast of the city. This natural ground cover is full of highly volatile oils and resins that burn quickly, especially when parched by low humidity and fanned by the seasonal Santa Ana winds.

In December 1924 Chief Ralph J. Scott urged the formation of the Mountain Patrol to protect sparsely populated but widespread mountain areas. Two Water Department buildings were converted into Mountain Patrol Stations along Mulholland Drive which ridges the top of the Santa Monica Mountains. Mountain Patrol No. 1 was located on the ridge at the intersection of Franklin and Coldwater Canyons while Mountain Patrol No. 2 was located farther west at Sepulveda Canyon. A third patrol was located at Fire Station 71 on Chalon Road at Stone Canyon. Additionally the Department built three lookout stations along the ridge, over 160 wooden water tanks, numerous remotely-located firefighting tool boxes, and a telephone communication system. Horses, autos, and small trucks were used to patrol the remote areas. In later years fixed wing aircraft were used for observation and then for water drops before helicopters came into use. Also developed was a large hose reel that rode the back of a tractor to lay hose in areas inaccessible to fire trucks.

The patrolmen wore distinctive uniforms of forest green with gray Stetson hats. Civilian employees of the patrol built and maintained 115 miles of firebreaks, 65 miles of trails, and 60 miles of fireroads. The patrolmen enforced fire ordinances, handled complaints, informed the public of fire safety, made property inspections, and assisted with fire fighting. They were aided with tank trucks, tractors, and water trailers to combat the fires.

The Mountain Patrol protected the Mountain Fire District until the fall of 1968 when increased residential development prompted construction of four fully staffed fire stations along Mulholland Drive. These stations were assisted by a brush unit with bulldozers which became the Wildland Fuel Management Unit we have today.

Units from the Mountain Patrol attack a mountain side brush fire.

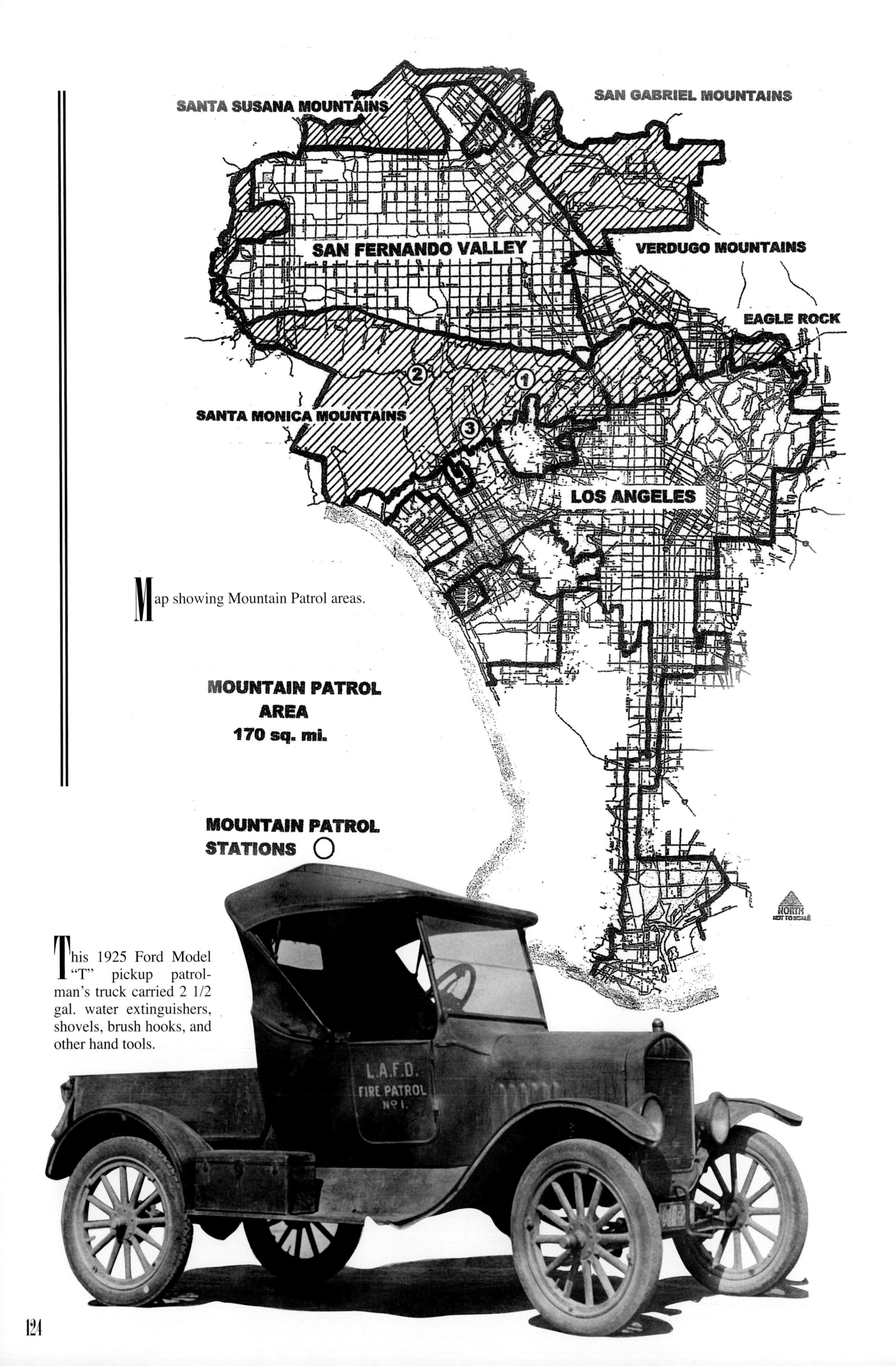

Map showing Mountain Patrol areas.

This 1925 Ford Model "T" pickup patrolman's truck carried 2 1/2 gal. water extinguishers, shovels, brush hooks, and other hand tools.

Another 1930 White fire patrol truck with a pump and equipment. One of several lookout towers is visible in the background.

Many in the entertainment business had homes in the mountain areas. Here is Humphrey Bogart with patrolmen who are erecting a no smoking sign in June of 1948. Each year similar signs were posted on the roads entering the brush areas to help prevent fires.

A 1930 White patrol truck with a front mounted 400 gpm pump, pulling a trailer-mounted water tank at Mountain Patrol No. 2.

The Mountain Patrol used trucks and horses to patrol the brush areas in 1930.

Patrol Station No. 1 used this 1930 White truck with a front mounted pump to fight fires in the mountain areas.

Above:
The patrol operated several lookout towers in the Santa Monica Mountains. Tower No. 2 was located on San Vicente Peak. At over 1900 feet, it was the highest point in the area. A patrolman poses here in 1940.

Left:
The LAFD shops built many pieces of equipment to adapt to fire fighting needs. This trailer mounted water tank, with pump, had tractor treads for rugged terrain. This unit was pulled by a tractor in the late 1920's.

A mounted patrolman at Patrol Station 2 in 1930.

The crew at Patrol Station No. 1 at 12601 Mulholland Drive with their 1925 Graham truck with a portable pump and a late 1920's Buick chief's car.

Here a Department of Water and Power truck is used by the Fire Department to transport firemen to a brush fire.

A fire crew cold-trailing a brush fire in the late 1930's.

Mountain Patrolman using the phone system on Mulholland Drive. The 1925 Model "T" with its fire fighting equipment was the patrol truck of that era.

The department developed this hose laying apparatus in 1954 on a D-8 Caterpillar tractor as it was too difficult to lay hose by hand in steep, heavy brush areas.

By 1957 the patrol was using these Ford one-ton pickups with hose tubs. The tubs held 300 feet of one inch hose and were easier and quicker than a hose reel to lay and reload without tangling.

Right:
To get their tractors to fire scenes the Mountain Patrol used tractor trailers like this 1932 Sterling.

Background photo:
A fixed-wing aircraft dropping a borate solution during the Bel Air Fire in 1961.

Mountain Patrol

A patrolman with his new 1933 Ford patrol truck.

In 1931 it snowed in the Santa Monica Mountains. Here is Mountain Patrol Station No. 1 in a winter wonderland.

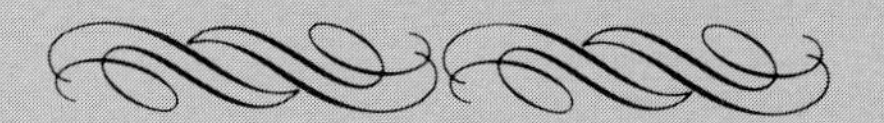

Chapter 9
Airports and Air Operations

AIRPORTS

The Los Angeles International airport (LAX) began as the Los Angeles Municipal airport in 1937. In 1928, the City Council selected 640 acres in Westchester for a proposed airport. It was named Mines Field for William Mines who was the real estate agent for the sale. The field was first used for air shows. In those days the entire airport consisted of one runway that ended east of Sepulveda Boulevard. The fire protection from 1930 to 1941 was provided by a volunteer engine company. The LAFD operated Fire Station 80 beginning in 1941 with a 1918 Seagrave engine. In 1943 a 1941 Mack crash truck was added. During World War II, the military took over the airport. After the war, the LAFD added equipment and built a new station as the airport expanded to meet the demands of popular commercial air travel.

Today's airport occupies 3425 acres, with four long runways, and is the fifth busiest airport in the world with over 60 million people traveling through each year. The LAFD has four stations in and around the airport with four state-of-the-art crash trucks.

Besides LAX, Los Angeles owns three other airports. The Ontario International airport, in San Bernardino County, acts as an alternate when LAX is shut down due to weather, safety, or security. The other airports are Palmdale Regional and Van Nuys. The Van Nuys airport was opened in 1928 but for private aircraft and manufacturing only. During the 1930's, it was used by the movie industry and was used as a backdrop for such movies as Casablanca. The Army took control of the airport during World War II for the training of pilots. They also expanded the runway and built many hangars. After the war, the city bought the airport for one dollar, since it was war surplus. Fire Station 90 was built in 1956 to house a task force and crash trucks.

AIR OPERATIONS

The department began Air Operations after the Bel Air fire in 1961 when they purchased their first helicopter, a Bell 47. Since then the fleet has grown to a total of six helicopters, most of which are Bell 412's. Besides use as observers and water droppers they also act as air ambulances and hoist rescues, assist with swift water rescues, and can deploy airborne engine companies to the rooftops of high-rise buildings. The helicopters are staffed 24 hours a day and are based in a 56,000 sq. ft. state of the art facility at the Van Nuys Airport.

The first LAFD helicopter put in service in April of 1962 was a Bell 47 three-seater. Known as Helicopter 1 it was involved in a crash June 23, 1974 which killed two firefighters. It is shown here at the far end of the line-up with the newer helicopters at Van Nuys Airport.

Above:

The LAFD also protects the Van Nuys Airport in the San Fernando Valley. Here, Crash 90 is seen laying a thick blanket of foam for a possible crash landing at the south end of the runway in 1969.

Right top:

Crash crews at a drill in 1964 at LAX with this Continental Airlines plane. Their practice would pay off when, in 1978, a DC-10 crashed during take-off killing three passengers. Crash 95 was a 1957 Yankee-FWD 6 x 6 truck. Crash 80 was a 1961 Yankee-FWD foam wagon and Tank Wagon 80 a 1958 Yankee-FWD.

Right Bottom:

While attempting to rescue survivors from a DC-6 which crash landed on a golf course south of the Van Nuys Airport, sparks from a power saw ignited fuel vapors. Two firefighters were seriously burned and six others were injured. The photo was taken just before the fuel vapor was ignited in February of 1976.

Right:

Helicopter Tender 2 was a 1979 Mack MB fuel tanker. It carried 2000 gallons of Jet-A aviation fuel to service the LAFD fleet.

Below:

In 1964 the crash crews from Fire Station 80 at LAX rolled out with this rig made by Walter-Yankee-FWD.

In 1948 this 1941 Mack crash wagon was part of the airport's firefighting force.

Before Los Angeles' airport became LAX it was a municipal airport known as Mines Field. The airport was protected by this 1940 GMC foam truck and a 1918 Seagrave chemical engine.

The water dropping helicopters see plenty of action in the dry hillsides around the city during the brush fire season.

Two crew members from Helicopter 1 balance on the skid as they pull an injured man aboard. The LAFD helicopter fire and rescue program was developed for the 1984 Summer Olympics which were held in Los Angeles. It is also a valuable tool for deploying personnel to areas of limited accessibility, such as mountain areas or roof tops.

Right:
Helicopter 6 surveys the damage caused by a brush fire in Laurel Canyon on September 16, 1979.

Chapter 10

Port of Los Angeles

For many years San Pedro Harbor was used by sailing ships trading with the Spanish settlers for beef hides and tallow. In the 1850's Phineas Banning began improving the bay as a port for Los Angeles, building a wharf in the shallow inner harbor at Wilmington and a wagon road to Los Angeles. In 1869 he built the first railroad in Southern California from the harbor to Los Angeles. The Southern Pacific Railroad gained control of this line in 1872 and extended it to San Pedro where a new deep water port was dredged.

The current port was established in 1907 and became part of the City of Los Angeles in 1909. Fire protection consisted of two contract tugboats and a few groups of volunteers with hand-drawn hose reels. In 1917, to supplement pumping volume, the Department loaded two horse-drawn steam engines onto a barge that was then towed to large fires. The first LAFD fireboat, the 25 foot Aeolian, was put in service in 1916. She was equipped with a 60 gallon chemical tank and a hose reel. The 64 foot wooden Los Angeles City Fireboat 1 was acquired in 1919 and could pump 2500 gpm. The largest and longest serving boat was Fireboat 2 constructed in 1925. In 1965 it was renamed the Ralph J. Scott. At 100 feet long, the steel ship had one of the first extendable water towers and could deliver over 13,000 gpm. Fireboat 3 was added in 1928 but at 38 feet and pumping 300 gpm, was used primarily as an auxiliary to the Scott. Fireboat 4 was added to the fleet in 1962. It was 76 feet long and could pump 9000 gpm. It was later named the Bethel F. Gifford. In 1967 and 1968 fireboats 1 and 3 were replaced and a new Fireboat 5 was purchased. When the venerable Ralph J. Scott was retired in 2003, she was replaced by a larger fireboat. The new Fireboat 2, the Warner L. Lawrence, is 105 feet long and can pump 38,000 gpm. That same year the small Fireboats 1, 3 and 5 were also replaced.

By 2006 the Port of Los Angeles had become the busiest container terminal in the country. The 7500 acre port has 43 miles of water front and serves over one million cruise ship passengers per year. Over $148 billion worth of cargo passed through the port in 2004. Besides containers, the port has facilities for bulk petroleum, vehicle imports, forest products, commercial and recreational vessels and for fuel and maintenance The port is now protected by four fireboat stations and five fireboats as well as several land based fire stations.

The Port also has a fire museum. Located on the first floor of San Pedro City Hall, the previous site of old Fire Station 36, it is operated by the LAFD Historical Society.

Fireboat 2 flies its commissioning flags in December of 1925. In 1965 it was renamed the Ralph J. Scott and retired in 2003. It served for 78 years and was the longest serving piece of apparatus in the LAFD.

Since the small fireboat Aeolian, put in service in 1916, did not have the needed pumping capacity for large fires, the LAFD stationed two steamers at Fire Station 36 that could be loaded on a barge. Here the steamers on the barge make short work of a lumber yard fire in San Pedro on Christmas day in 1919.

In the rear of Fireboat 2's quarters was a station for motorized apparatus which became Fire Station 112. Boat tenders operated out of this station and carried large amounts of large capacity hose and a boat monitor. This 1925 Mack hose wagon provided the hose to permit the fireboats to supply saltwater many blocks inland for fighting fires.

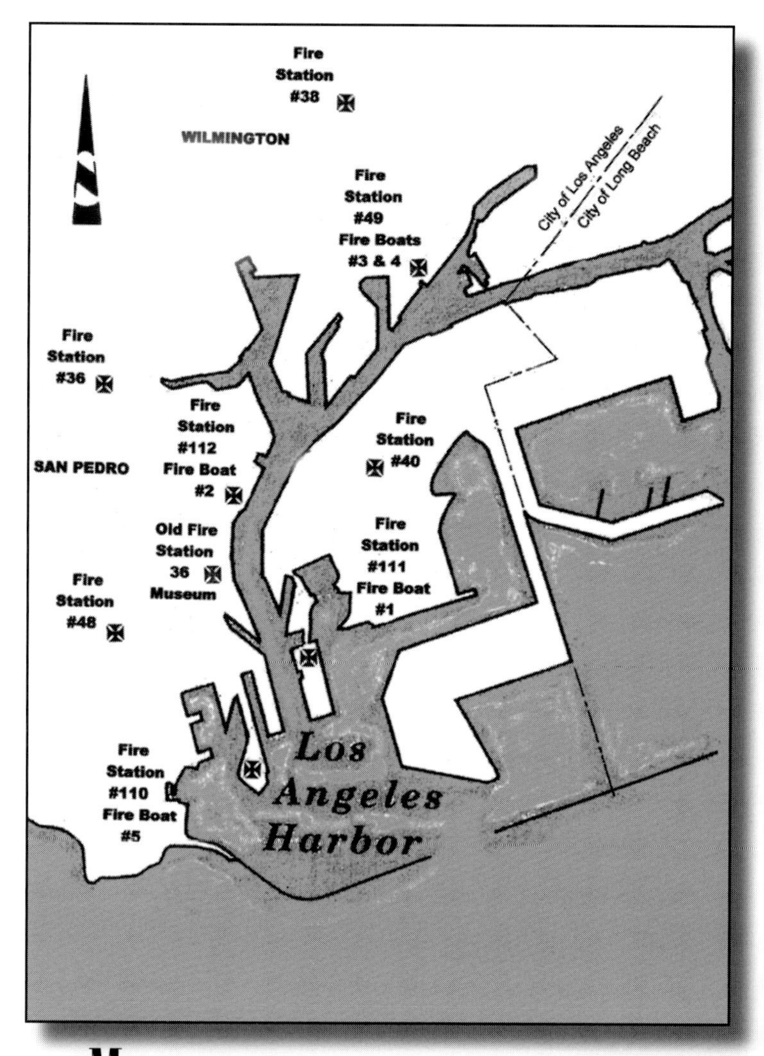

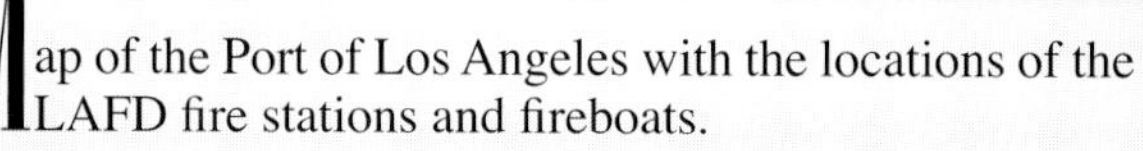

Map of the Port of Los Angeles with the locations of the LAFD fire stations and fireboats.

To keep an iron fireboat going in salt water for 78 years requires constant maintenance and the dedication of hundreds of firefighters during its active life.

Fireboat 1, built in 1919, at its station at the foot of First Street in San Pedro in the early twenties.

The first fire protection on the waterfront consisted of two contracted tugboats, the Warrior and the Falcon, equipped with fire fighting monitors. *(Above Left)*

Fireboat 4 arrived at the port on February 22, 1962 with flags and water flying. Affectionately known as the White Swan, it would later be named the Bethel F. Gifford and have its hull painted red. *(Above Center)*

Engine 53's crew cools an adjacent tank at this Union Oil tank farm fire on July 12, 1951. Several tanks were involved before the fire was brought under control. *(Below)*

In 1961 the LAFD developed a system of fighting wharf fires by using scuba equipped firefighters under the wharf. During a drill, four divers launch an attack from the deck of Fireboat 3 using a 2 1/2 inch floating monitor and two 1 1/2 inch floating monitors. *(Above Right)*

A textbook attack on a wharf fire at the Harbor Grain Terminal at Berth 174 on December 28, 1967. The big boats, 2 and 4, cut off the extension, while the smaller Boat 5 acts as a command and safety vessel. Other boats will place water curtains at each end and deploy scuba divers to provide the final extinguishment. *(Below)*

Above:

Crews from Engines 85 and 101 attack a stubborn wharf fire in January 1988 using handlines and access ports in the wharf deck. With help from the fireboats and the scuba divers, the damage was held to 250 feet of wharf, six fishing boats, and two piles of nets.

Left Center:

Engine Company 36 at its station in the old City of San Pedro City Hall at 630 South Beacon Street in 1919. The apparatus was a 1914 American LaFrance 700 gpm double combination pumper and hose. Battalion Chief John C. Baly and friend lead the way.

Left Bottom:

Engine 36 in front of Fire Station 40 at 406 Tuna Street on Terminal Island. The building, originally occupied by Hose Company 5, was moved to this site from 1439 West Vernon Avenue in 1920.

On June 22, 1947 the tanker S.S. Markay exploded and burned. The fire spread across Slip 1 and ignited the wharf at Berth 150-155. Fireboat 2 had to blast its way through smoke and flame to protect the upper reaches of the slip.

Fireboat 2 opens up with her big guns at a ship fire drill. The vessel was slated to be scrapped.

Fireboat 2 in action at the December 17, 1976 explosion and fire aboard the Liberian tanker M.V. Sansinena. Nine people were killed and many more were rescued by the crews of Fireboats 3 and 5.

Fireboat 2 rests easy in the boathouse at Berth 227 in the Port of Los Angeles. It resided in this house for 60 years, from July 1926 until July 3, 1986.

Fireboat 4 greets the dawn and inspects the desolation on the morning after the explosion and fire.

Chapter 11
Rescue Services

Rescue service began in 1927 when the Department put a 1922 White rescue squad in service at Fire Station 23. This initial service was to provide breathing apparatus and medical aid to firemen at fire scenes. By 1930, LAFD ambulances were in service to transport injured firemen to hospitals. This service was soon extended to the public in the Central and Harbor areas. From the mid 1930's to 1970, the public ambulance service in the Central area was operated by the Police Department and the Receiving Hospitals. They operated a fleet of brown vans that were housed at each Police Station. Private ambulance companies provided rescue service in the San Fernando Valley and in West Los Angeles. The LAFD started rescue ambulance service in the San Fernando Valley in 1955. In 1970, the Fire Department replaced the Police ambulance system in the rest of the city. By 1978, there were 37 LAFD rescue ambulances in operation throughout the city.

Two 1920 Studebaker rescue trucks at the back door of Fire Station 23 on Winston Street. Although Fire Station 23 has only one apparatus door, the station is a block long. The engine and truck respond out the front on Fifth Street while the rescue trucks leave from the back on Winston Street.

In 1930 this Studebaker was assigned to rescue service at Fire Station 23.

Rescue 2 , a 1928 GMC, with its equipment at the drill tower.

Rescue Services

This 1950 Mack heavy utility was assigned to Fire Station 27 in 1951. In 1974 it was operating out of Fire Station 88 in Sherman Oaks.

Rescue 1, a 1925 Dodge, assigned to Station 23 at 225 East Fifth Street. Early rescue trucks supplied breathing apparatus to firefighters but did not transport the injured to hospitals until 1930.

A classic 1938 LaSalle ambulance, first assigned to Fire Station 3. The equipment includes an E & J Resuscitator, an H &H Inhalator, self-contained oxygen masks, a first aid kit, and other rescue tools. The ambulance was later assigned to Fire Station 27 in Hollywood as shown here.

On the right is a 1928 White assigned to the shops. It was replaced by the 1948 Kenworth heavy utility with a Holmes twin boom tow crane with a 20 ton capacity. It was equipped with power take-offs, an air compressor, jack hammers, pneumatic tools, oxy-acetylene cutting tools, and other rescue tools. It operated out of Fire Station 14 at 3401 South Central Avenue.

Two 1936 Ford rescue vehicles. Rescue 36 served the San Pedro area from Fire Station 36 on Beacon Street.

Right:

This 1928 Studebaker was lettered as Rescue 1 and appears outside Fire Station 16 on Hope Street.

Below:

Paramedic rescue ambulance service began in the San Pedro/Harbor area on July 29, 1968 with this International built for ambulance service. It was stationed at Fire Station 53 on Mesa Street in San Pedro.

These Ford Club Wagon van type ambulances were used to accommodate two patients lying down or one lying down and six sitting up. These units were manned by civilian emergency medical technicians.

Rescue Services

Crown also made heavy utilities as shown by this 1968 model. It ran out of Fire Station 6 on Edgeware Road near Downtown Los Angeles.

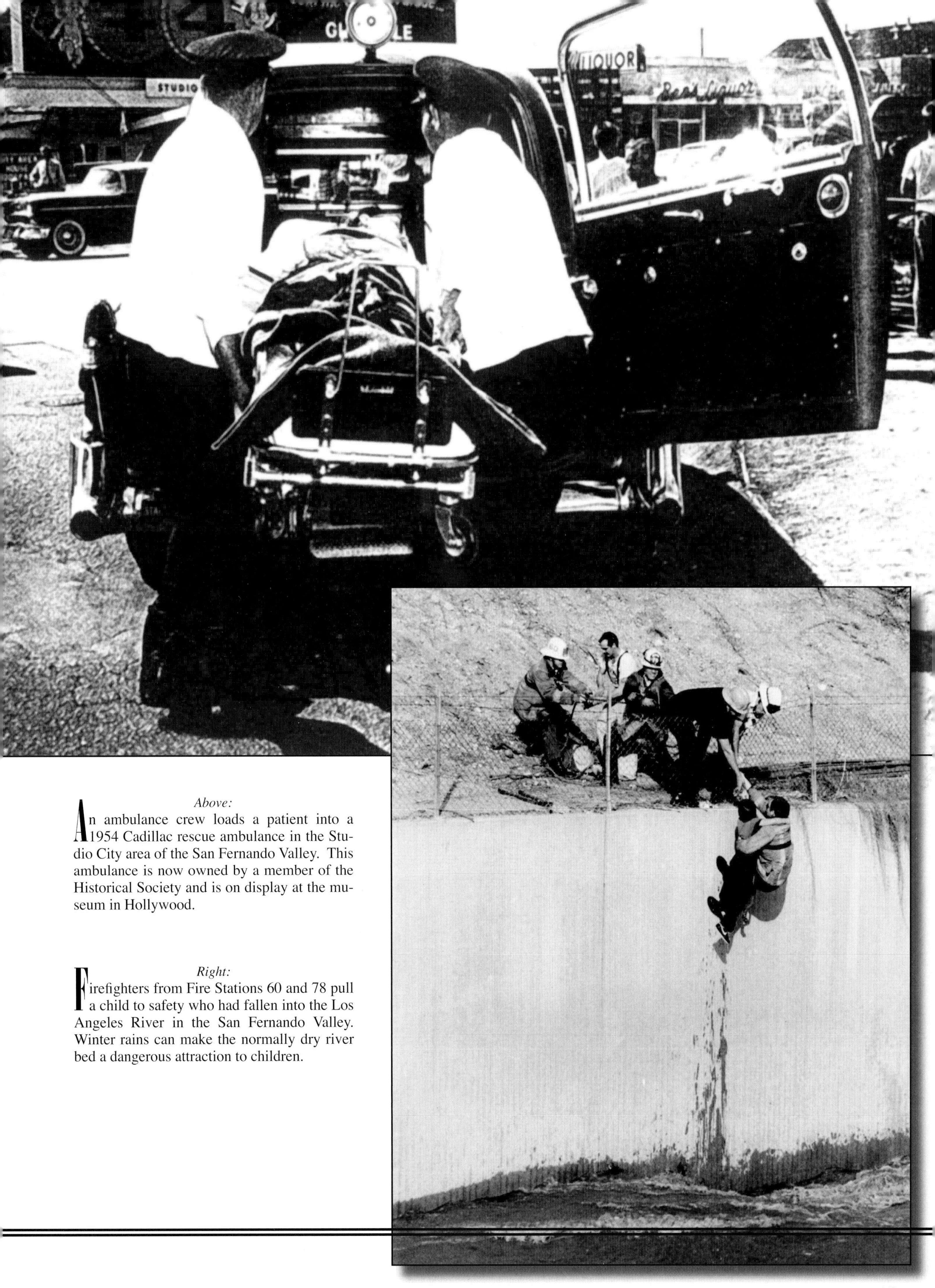

Above:

An ambulance crew loads a patient into a 1954 Cadillac rescue ambulance in the Studio City area of the San Fernando Valley. This ambulance is now owned by a member of the Historical Society and is on display at the museum in Hollywood.

Right:

Firefighters from Fire Stations 60 and 78 pull a child to safety who had fallen into the Los Angeles River in the San Fernando Valley. Winter rains can make the normally dry river bed a dangerous attraction to children.

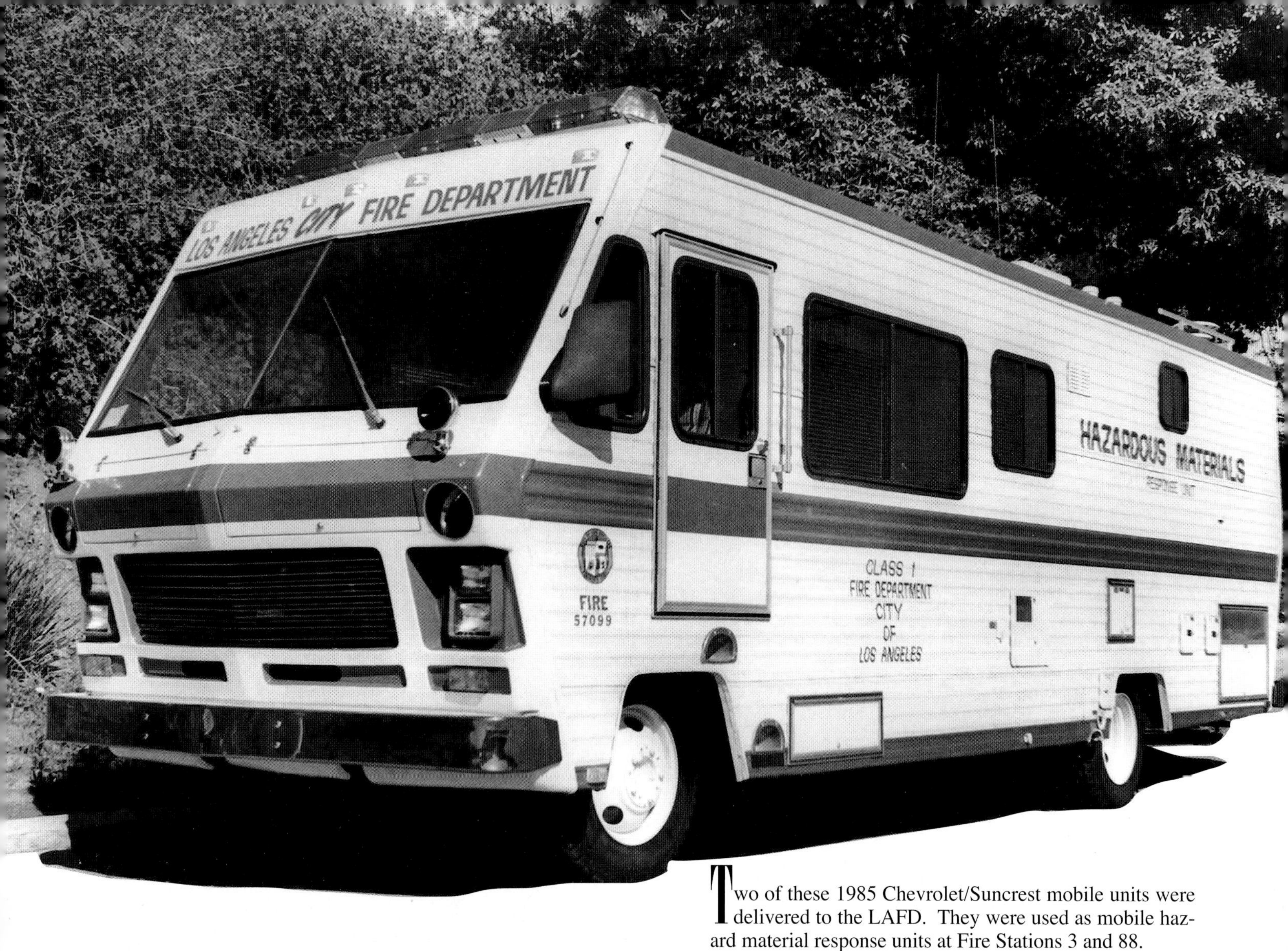

Two of these 1985 Chevrolet/Suncrest mobile units were delivered to the LAFD. They were used as mobile hazard material response units at Fire Stations 3 and 88.

This is one of seven 1968 Chevrolet Yankee ambulances that were purchased for service in the San Fernando Valley.

Chapter 12

Support Services

SIGNAL OFFICES

From 1883 until 1925, all fire alarms were dispatched from the old city hall. In 1925, the Westlake Signal Office opened and was the central dispatch center until 1973. There were smaller signal offices in outlying areas such as San Pedro, West Los Angeles, Van Nuys, and at Mountain Patrol No. 1. Most of these were replaced when the Coldwater Signal Office was built in 1963. Radios were not installed in Department vehicles until 1946. The first to receive radios were the chiefs' cars and the fireboats. The current dispatch center, located in City Hall East, replaced all of the other signal offices in 1973.

TRAINING

The first drill tower was built in 1887 in Downtown Los Angeles. In 1911, a second tower was built at the department shops at Avenue 19 and Pasadena Avenue. By 1930, this wooden tower was replaced by a more modern concrete one. Now drill towers and training centers are located at several regional Fire Stations and at the Frank Hotchkin Memorial Training Center in Elysian Park.

SHOPS

The original department shops were built at Avenue 19 and Pasadena Avenue in the late 1800's to maintain the horse-drawn equipment and to provide care for the horses. The shops were improved and expanded through the years to meet the needs of the motorized department and to build special equipment. By 1960, the old shops were replaced by a modern complex of concrete buildings at the same location. Today the shops maintain over 1000 Fire Department vehicles, helicopters, and boats.

FIRE PREVENTION & PUBLIC SAFETY

Fire prevention started with the founding of the department in 1886. In those days, in order to prevent fires, ordinances were passed that limited the amount of hay and kerosene that could be stored in a building. A hydrant section was formed in 1891 to provide sources of water for fire fighting. The first hydrants were manhole accesses into the zanja water ditches and pipelines. By 2006 there were over 59,000 fire hydrants in the city. In 1921 a fire prevention bureau was established to perform inspections of property and educate the public on fire safety.

Left:
Shown is the inside of the Westlake Signal Office, where all Department activity is marked with magnets on a wall map. Each magnet represents a company either in quarters or responding to an incident. When too many magnets are absent from a fire station location, the Floor Captain knows to send a move-up company to that Fire Station.

Right
A civilian points to the location of a fire for Engine Co. 17 after pulling a corner alarm box. Alarm boxes were used frequently to report fires until telephones became more widely used. There were about 50 alarm boxes in the city in 1886. By 1975 all of the alarm boxes were removed.

The Westlake Signal Office was the central dispatch center from 1925 to 1973. It was located on the north side of Westlake Park, now known as MacArthur Park. Dispatching is now done by Operations Control Dispatch Section (OCD) located on the fourth sub-level of City Hall East.

The LAFD used this 1924 White bus to transport firemen recruits to the training facilities at the new drill tower built in 1930.

Fire Department recruits learn to rely on pompier ladders when ground ladders are too short to reach the desired floor. Because it was impossible to carry anyone down a pompier ladder, rope was always carried to lower rescued victims. The old wooden drill tower was built in 1911 and was located at the shops on Avenue 19 and Pasadena Avenue.

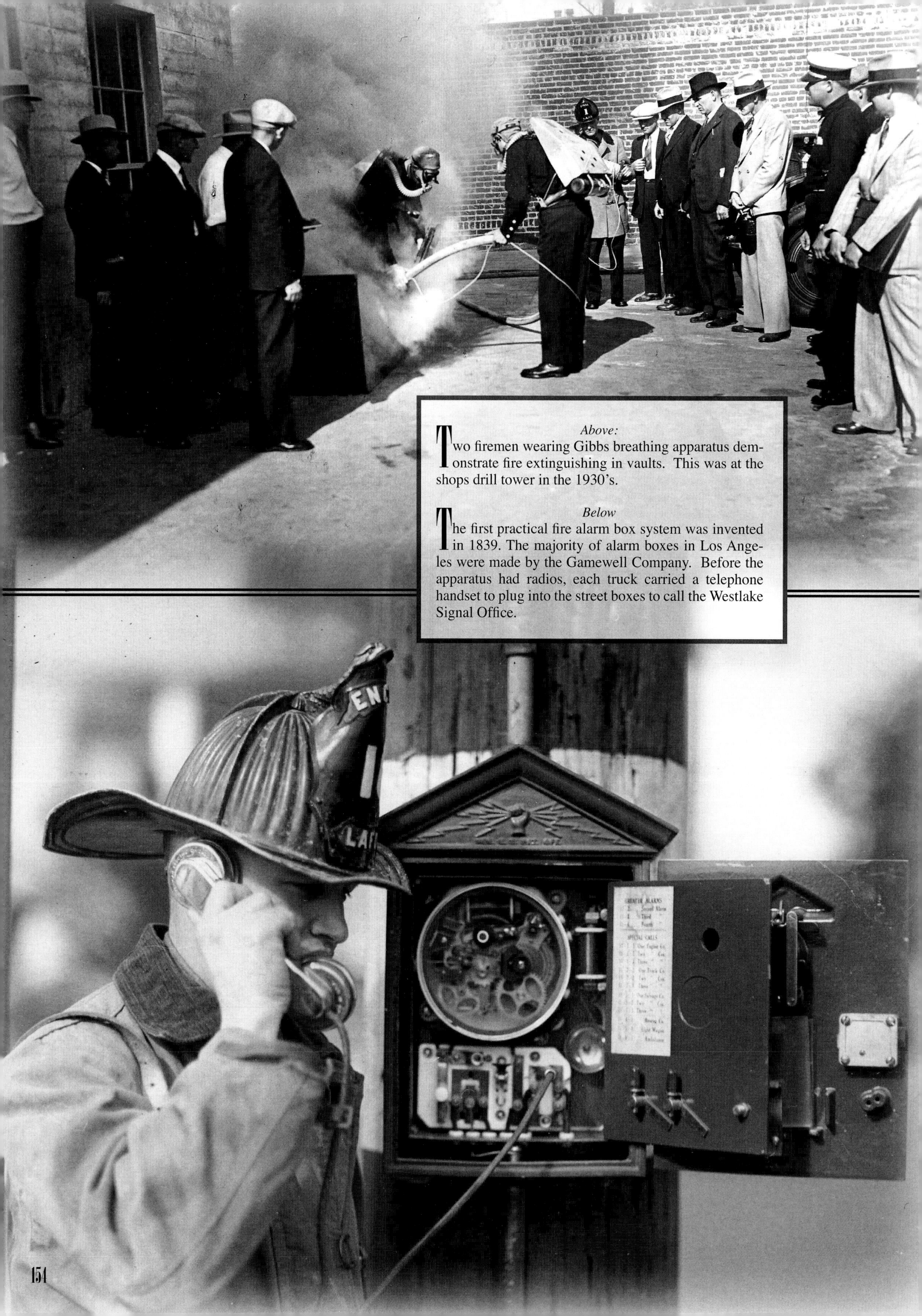

Above:

Two firemen wearing Gibbs breathing apparatus demonstrate fire extinguishing in vaults. This was at the shops drill tower in the 1930's.

Below

The first practical fire alarm box system was invented in 1839. The majority of alarm boxes in Los Angeles were made by the Gamewell Company. Before the apparatus had radios, each truck carried a telephone handset to plug into the street boxes to call the Westlake Signal Office.

Above:

Fire Department personnel kept the fire hydrants painted bright yellow. There were about 20,000 hydrants in Los Angeles in 1933. Today there are over 59,000 fire hydrants in the city.

Right:

Extensive training by the recruits at the concrete drill tower in 1942.

Below:

Door to door inspections of residences by fire companies began in 1951. Here Engine 35, with their 1948 Mack high pressure hose wagon and 1945 Kenworth pump, perform the inspections in their Hollywood district.

Left:
Mechanics servicing two engines and a salvage truck inside the old shops in the 1950's.

Below:
The new shops featured multiple repair bays and modern equipment as shown here in the 1970's.

The Coldwater Signal Office opened in 1963 to dispatch fire companies in the San Fernando Valley, West Los Angeles, and Westchester, including LAX. The signal office was located on Mulholland Drive east of Coldwater Canyon Boulevard and was in service until 1973. In 1977, the Signal Office became Fire Station 108.

Right:
Graduation exercises at the Frank Hotchkin Memorial Training Center drill tower in May of 2006.

Arson investigator searching for the cause of a fire. If arson is suspected it is their job to locate and arrest the arsonist.

Arson: Start a fire...go to jail! Arson investigators are peace officers with full power to make arrests. They wear civilian clothing, carry handcuffs and a gun, and drive unmarked police-type cars.

Chapter 13
Modernization

With the end of the 20th century approaching the department purchased modern apparatus and increased the use of helicopters. This period saw the last of the open cab apparatus and the entrance of the fully enclosed crew cab units. Ladder trucks now featured enclosed cabs for the tiller positions. Gone too, was the practice of personnel riding on the tailboards.

No less than five ladder pipes poured water on this fire at the Ontra Cafeteria on Vine Street in 1990. The building had been declared an historical landmark by the City Council but was vacant for two years before the fire.

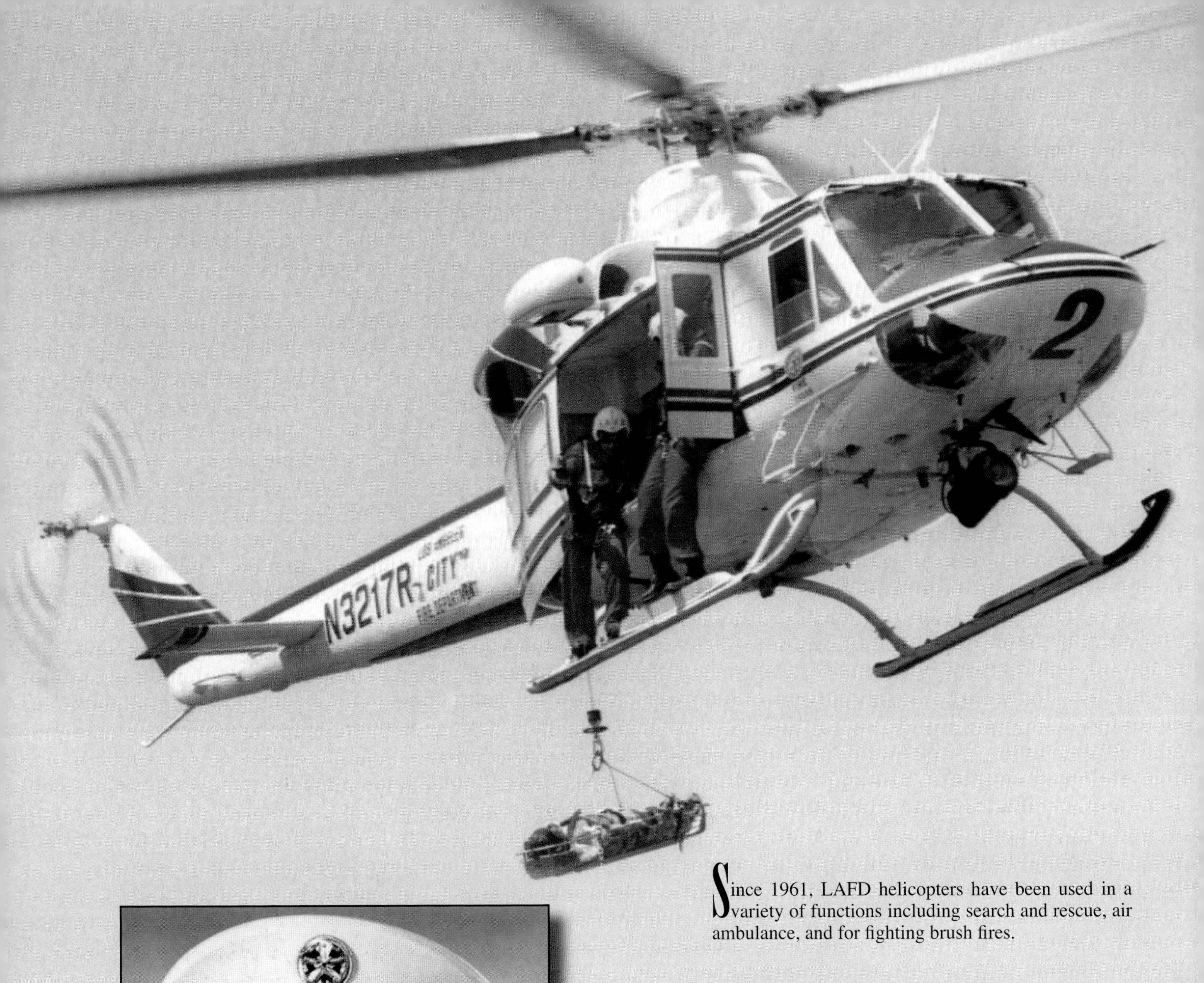

Since 1961, LAFD helicopters have been used in a variety of functions including search and rescue, air ambulance, and for fighting brush fires.

Modernization

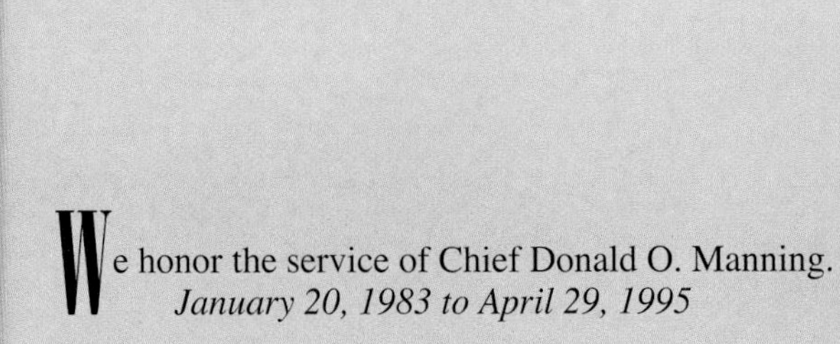

We honor the service of Chief Donald O. Manning.
January 20, 1983 to April 29, 1995

This 1992 fire occurred on the seventh floor of the Los Angeles County Health Building at 313 North Figueroa Street. It took 46 fire companies to bring the fire under control.

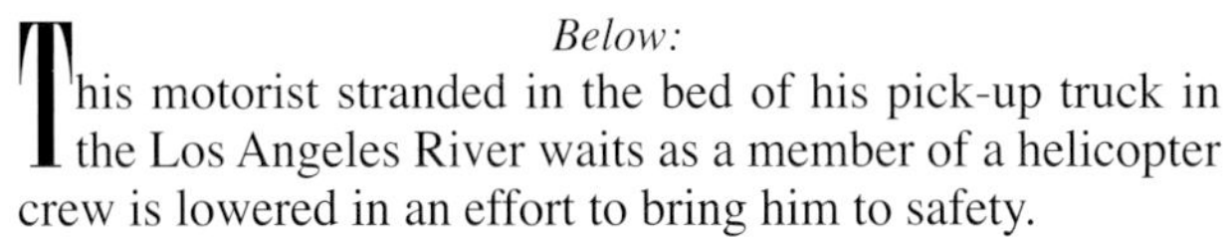

Below:
This motorist stranded in the bed of his pick-up truck in the Los Angeles River waits as a member of a helicopter crew is lowered in an effort to bring him to safety.

Engine and Truck 29 get a washdown in front of old Fire Station 29, which was built in 1912 at 158 South Western Avenue. A new Fire Station 29 was completed in 1991 at 4029 Wilshire Boulevard.

Above:

LAFD helicopter Fire 4 on patrol over the Hollywood Hills. All the department helicopters are stationed at Air Operations headquarters, Fire Station 114, at the Van Nuys Airport.

Left:

Helicopter 3 makes a water drop on a hillside brush fire.

Below:

Los Angeles bought eighteen of these 1998 Pierce Dash triples. This one is supplying water for the helicopters at a brush fire near Porter Ranch in the North San Fernando Valley.

Modernization

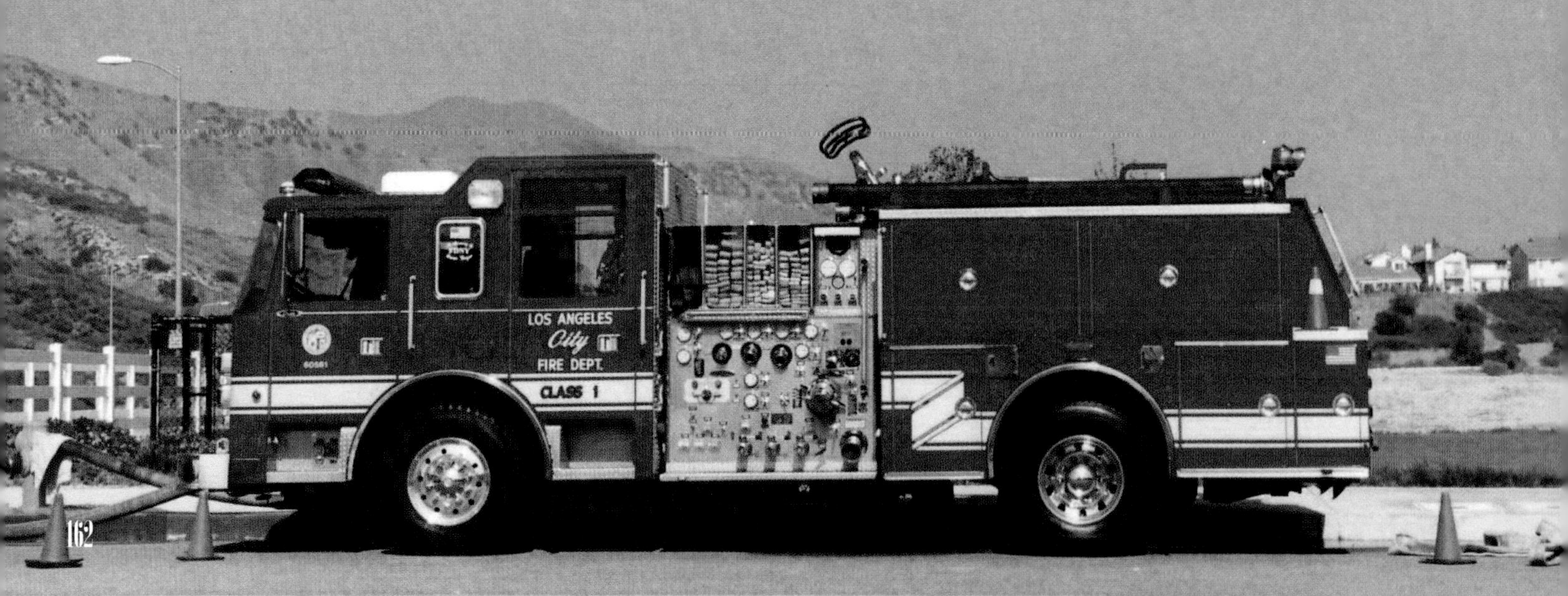

A fire at the Terry Lumber Company yard at 3250 North San Fernando Road took twenty-three fire companies an hour and a half to knock down.

With the flames roaring from a structure a few feet away, the chief takes time out to check burgers on the grill.

While transporting an eleven year old child to Children's Hospital Los Angeles, LAFD helicopter Fire 3 crashed in Griffith Park on March 23, 1998. The child and three fire-fighters were killed while two other rescue personnel survived but suffered serious injuries.

Engine 82 stationed at 1800 North Bronson Avenue is one of the companies protecting the Hollywood area. The first Sea-grave triple with an automatic transmission purchased by the LAFD was one of these 1980 engines.

The crew from Fire Station 90 uses the Jaws of Life to free the driver from this serious traf-fic accident in the San Fernando Valley.

Emergency Air No. 1 responded to greater alarm fires with its load of air bottles to replenish the breathing apparatus worn by the firefighters. This 1983 White also contains a compressor to refill the bottles.

This light utility vehicle was an indispensable tool at night fire scenes. The portable unit could be raised for use or lowered for travel.

One of 41 1984 Seagrave 1500 gpm triples purchased by LAFD.

There is no limit to the type of rescues performed by the Air Operations Division of the LAFD. They are shown here during a rocky ocean shore rescue.

The six helicopters of the LAFD cover the 469 square miles of Los Angeles from the mountains to the ocean.

Right on the mark! An LAFD helicopter lays a water drop on a brush fire in the foothills of Los Angeles.

Fire companies from all over Los Angeles responded to this early morning fire at a restaurant in Porter Ranch in 1999.

100 foot flames lick at firefighters as they attempt to stop a brush fire in the rocky hills above Chatsworth in the northwest portion of the San Fernando Valley.

The LAFD answers many calls for fires and accidents on the freeways that crisscross the city.

Parking can be a problem in Los Angeles! A variety of apparatus including Crowns, Seagraves, and Ward LaFrances responded to the fire at the Ontra Cafeteria.

This 1993 Seagrave triple combination pumper was the first of nine to be delivered to the Department.

On March 24, 1985 methane gas seeping underground was ignited and the resulting explosion destroyed a clothing store at Third Street and Ogden Drive. Flames shot from cracks in nearby sidewalks, curbs, and pavement.

Chapter 14

Today's Department

The Crew of Engine 60 advance a hose line as they prepare to attack a well involved structure.

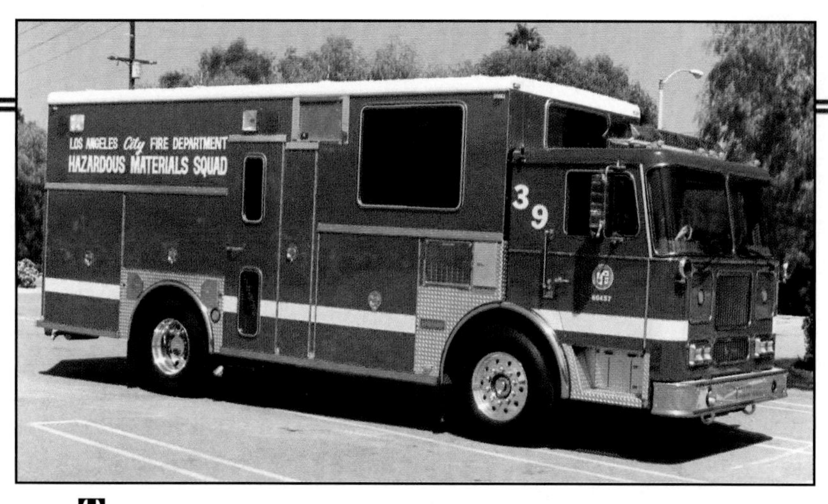

This 1992 Seagrave/Saulsbury squad from Fire Station 39 in Van Nuys was one of three purchased for the city.

Today's Department

We honor the service of Fire Chief William Bamattre.
April 30, 1995 to present

When motorists try to beat the train to a crossing it can be deadly as shown here near a crossing in Fire Station 89's first-in district.

Two of these 1979 Oshkosh crash trucks were purchased by the city and were assigned to Foam 1-80 and Foam 2-80 at the Los Angeles International Airport (LAX).

LAX is protected by two of these 1998 Emergency One airport crash rescue apparatus. Both operate out of Fire Station 80.

Seven of these Ford F-350 4 x 4's are used in the mountain areas as patrol trucks. This unit is assigned to Fire Station 99 on Mulholland Drive.

Today's Department

In July of 2005 the LAFD began displaying this colorful new shoulder patch.

A firefighter from Task Force 60 finds himself all alone as he is confronted by two fully involved residences. The fire in the San Fernando Valley was brought under control in about 30 minutes.

How about a nice cool shower instead of hot smoke and flames! Firefighters from Light Force 28 are soaked as they try to deflect the flow of water by pushing the car that knocked off the fire hydrant back over it. The effort failed as the water pressure was too great. The house behind was badly damaged from the water flow.

The end of an era is marked by the lifting out of the water of retired Fireboat 2, the Ralph J. Scott. It served the LAFD for 78 years and plans are underway to preserve the vessel in a permanent museum at the harbor.

Graduating recruits participate in a wet drill at the Frank Hotchkin Memorial Training Center drill tower in Elysian Park.

Above:

Fire Station 27, next door to the LAFDHS Museum in Hollywood, received one of the seven 2003 American LaFrance 100 foot, enclosed tiller ladder trucks.

Right:

The LAFD purchased 18 of these Pierce Dash pumpers in 1998 and 1999 to replace an aging fleet.

Below:

Urban Search and Rescue 27 operates this 1999 Dash 2000 diesel truck.

These 2003 rehab/air tenders are stationed at Fire Stations 28, 59, and 85. They carry spare air bottles, an air compressor, a toilet, a shower, food and water, plus a light tower.

Right

The department has two of these Freightliner command units shown here at the Valley Shops. They are stationed at Fire Stations 3 and 88.

Above:

Helicopter Tender 2, a 2001 Freightliner, carries 3800 gallons of Jet-A fuel for the helicopters at Van Nuys Airport.

The majority of calls to the department are for rescue ambulances. The LAFD has at least one ambulance at every fire station. This is one of the new Ford/Wheeledcoach ambulances.

Heavy Rescue 56 and an urban search and rescue unit on the scene of an apartment building collapse in Echo Park in December of 2000.

Four 1999 Freightliner/Pierce foam tenders are in service around the city at Fire Stations 17, 86, 100, and 112.

Right:

Heavy Rescue 56, a 2002 Peterbilt, is equipped with a 40 ton crane with a 360 degree operation.

Below:

Swift water rescue team members and Heavy Rescue 56 remove a badly damaged car from the Los Angeles River.

Fire Station 112 at Berth 85 in San Pedro has been the home of Fireboat 2, the Ralph J. Scott and the new Warner L. Lawrence since 1986.

Fireboat 1, located at Station 111 on Terminal Island, is one of three new 40 foot boats operated by the department. They replaced the 36 foot fiberglass boats 1, 3, and 5.

Dedication ceremonies were held in April of 2003 as the mayor of Los Angeles christened the new Boat 2, the Warner L. Lawrence, while aboard the retiring Ralph J. Scott. Note the huge difference in size.

Top:

New Fire Station 28 was built by a subdivision developer at 11641 Corbin Avenue in the Porter Ranch area in 1993. Although some department functions used the station starting in 1994, Light Force 28 did not move in until the year 2000.

Center:

One of the latest stations to open was 77's at 9224 Sunland Boulevard in Sun Valley. This new station, as well as other new stations, offer apparatus doors on two streets and room for expansion.

The 100 year old Los Angeles Firemen's Relief Association has expanded to include assistance for not only the widows, orphans, and disabled firefighters but also provides life insurance, off duty sick and injury benefits and a death benefit for burial of deceased active and retired members. Communication between the Relief Association and the active and retired membership is provided by the monthly publication known as the Firemen's Grapevine.

Below

Fire Station 68, built in 1987, on West Washington Boulevard.

Two truck company members begin opening the roof of this scorching attic fire on Cahuenga Boulevard.

Today's Department

New Los Angeles Fireboat 2, the Warner L. Lawrence, in the open sea outside of the Los Angeles Harbor in 2003 on its arrival from Seattle.

This photo at Fire Station 112 depicts the theme of the LAFD, on land, sea and air.

Air ambulance operations are a major part of the Air Operations Division (Air Ops) of the LAFD. A helicopter can transport a critical patient to a hospital within a few minutes. Seen here is a Bell 412 airship.

Firefighters and helicopter crew members prepare to load an injured child aboard Fire 2, in preparation for a flight to Children's Hospital.

The swift water units respond to water rescues in the Los Angeles River which runs from the San Fernando Valley to San Pedro. This unit is a 2003 Ford F-450 4 x 4 and is one of four units in the city.

New Fire Station 61 at 5821 West Third Street was completed in 1986.

Above:

The LAFD uses two of these 1995 Hummer 4 x 4's as brush patrol units. Fire Station 109 is at the former site of Mountain Patrol 2.

Left:

It does not matter how long a firefighter has been on the job, he is always saddened to see child victims of fire.

Below:

Like a mother hen with her chicks, new Boat 2, the Warner L. Lawrence, poses with new boats 1, 3, and 5.

Above:

Fire Station 87's small 1951 quarters on Balboa Boulevard in the North San Fernando Valley will soon be replaced by this new station, under construction, at 10124 Balboa Boulevard. The new station will also serve as a community center and a meeting place for the Community Emergency Response Team (CERT).

Left:

First built as a station for horse-drawn apparatus in 1904 at 2669 West Pico Boulevard, Fire Station 13 was relocated to South Vermont Avenue in 1950. This artist's rendition shows how the new Station 13 will look when built at Pico and Westmoreland in the near future.

Fire Station 83 was originally located at 16593 Ventura Boulevard in 1942 and housed only a tank wagon. In 1948 it was relocated to Balboa Boulevard in Encino. This spacious new station was opened in 2006 at 4960 Balboa Boulevard.

Chapter 15
The Museum and Memorial

The museum was an idea that took many years to become a reality. The LAFD Historical Society (LAFDHS) planned for years to use Fire Station 27 when it was vacated by the Department. In 1992 it was replaced by a new station on Cole Avenue, just south of the old station. However, the 1994 Northridge Earthquake changed everything when it caused heavy damage to the masonry building. After a major reconstruction, with a great deal of steel reinforcement, it was opened as a museum on October 11, 2001.

The LAFDHS is constructing a Fallen Firefighter Memorial to honor members who lost their lives in the line of duty. The memorial being built in front of the museum will contain five bronze statues depicting the LAFD in action at an incident where a firefighter has been injured. An arched wall behind the statues will contain the names of the fallen firefighters. The entire area will be paved with brick pavers which will be engraved with the names of individuals or organizations who donated to the memorial project. The bricks are laid out as a map of Hollywood upon which is superimposed an outline of the city of Los Angeles with designations for freeways and fire stations. Inside the museum is a Wall of Flame honoring donors for their contributions to the memorial.

Old Fire Station 27 , at 1355 North Cahuenga Boulevard in Hollywood with new Fire Station 27 on the left. The old station, built in 1930, was the largest fire station west of the Mississippi River at that time. It is now the home of the LAFD Historical Society Museum and the William Rolland Firefighters Educational Institute.

Old Fire Station 27 in the 1970's when Crown fire apparatus were popular.

On October 13, 1960, Fireman Bob Foster, Truck 17B, was declared the Department's Official Historian by the Fire Commission. Foster (second from right) had spent much of his own time, money, and effort researching and recording historical events of the LAFD. Left to right are Chief William Miller, Commissioner J. Richard Sneed, President of the Commission Harold R. Billings, Foster, and Commission Vice President Roy H. Sheldon.

Fire safety instruction at the William Rolland Firefighters' Institute at the museum.

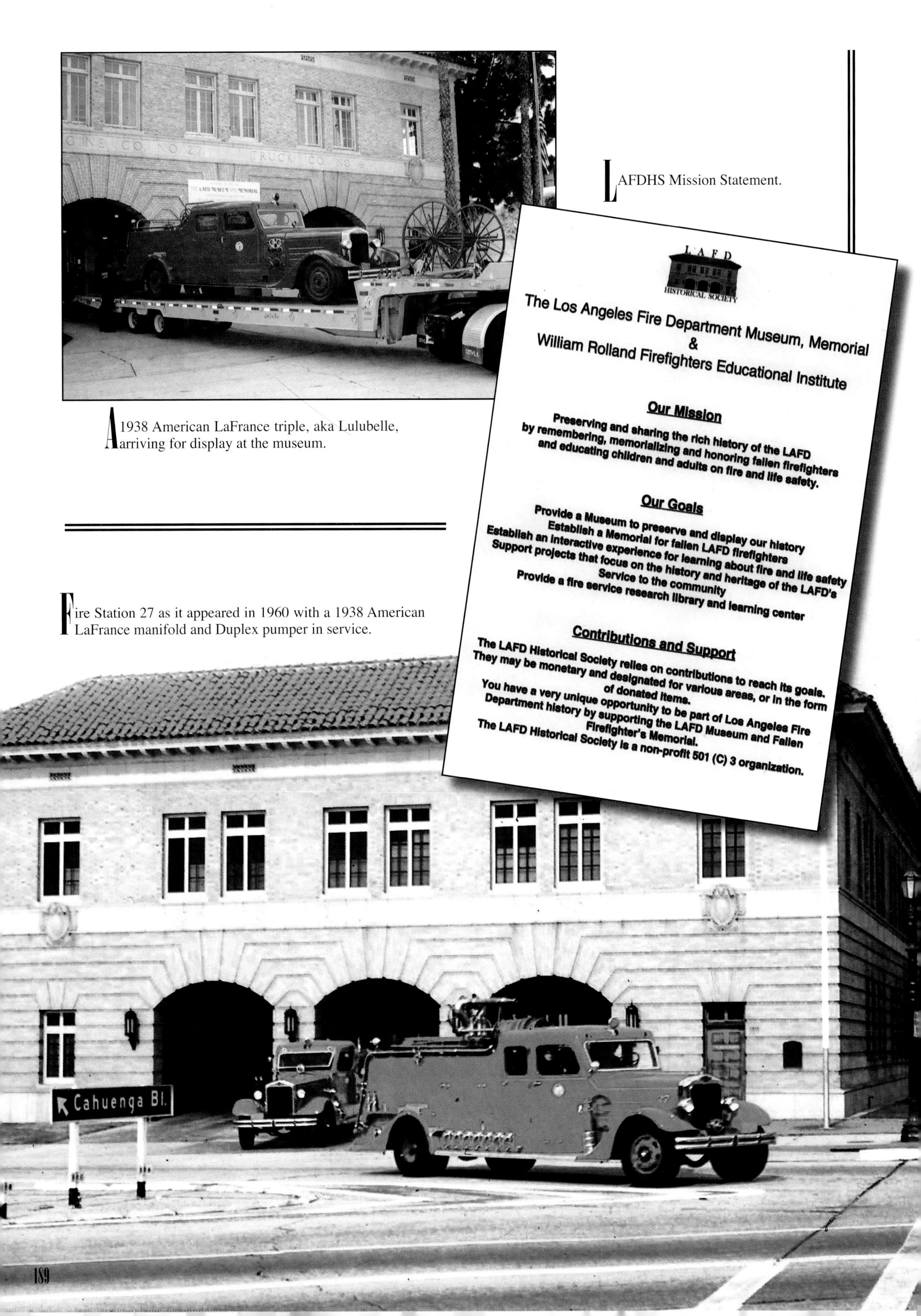

A 1938 American LaFrance triple, aka Lulubelle, arriving for display at the museum.

LAFDHS Mission Statement.

L A F D
HISTORICAL SOCIETY

The Los Angeles Fire Department Museum, Memorial
&
William Rolland Firefighters Educational Institute

Our Mission

Preserving and sharing the rich history of the LAFD by remembering, memorializing and honoring fallen firefighters and educating children and adults on fire and life safety.

Our Goals

Provide a Museum to preserve and display our history
Establish a Memorial for fallen LAFD firefighters
Establish an interactive experience for learning about fire and life safety
Support projects that focus on the history and heritage of the LAFD's Service to the community
Provide a fire service research library and learning center

Contributions and Support

The LAFD Historical Society relies on contributions to reach its goals. They may be monetary and designated for various areas, or in the form of donated items.

You have a very unique opportunity to be part of Los Angeles Fire Department history by supporting the LAFD Museum and Fallen Firefighter's Memorial.

The LAFD Historical Society is a non-profit 501 (C) 3 organization.

Fire Station 27 as it appeared in 1960 with a 1938 American LaFrance manifold and Duplex pumper in service.

The Los Angeles Fire Department's Medal of Valor is presented to members who perform an act of conspicuous heroism and/or bravery under extreme personal risk in the line of duty.

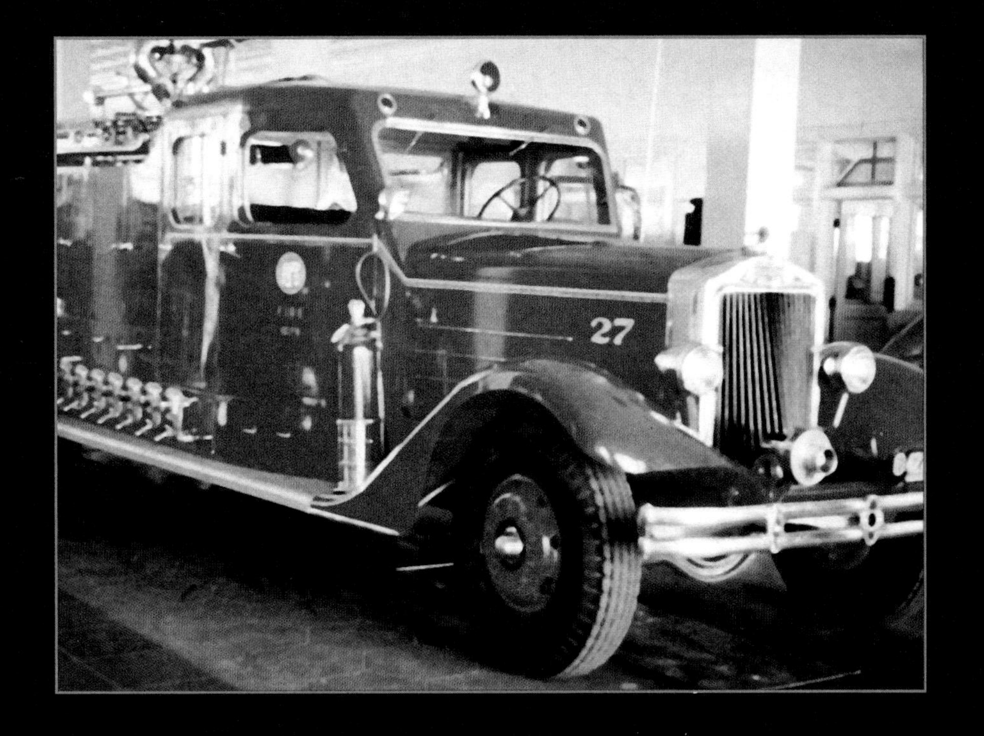

A 1938 American LaFrance manifold wagon on the apparatus floor of old Fire Station 27 in the 1950's. The manifold wagon could provide up to fourteen 2 1/2 inch hose lines and a boat sized monitor at a fire.

Below:
The station that housed Engine 27 and Truck 9 from 1913 to 1930 burned in 1979. It was located a few blocks north of the museum at 1625 North Cahuenga Boulevard.

The Museum and Memorial

There are currently nine vehicles on display at the museum. When the station opened in 1930 it housed a dozen vehicles. This is the apparatus floor of the museum with three of the nine vehicles visible.

One of the many equipment and helmet displays at the museum. There are over 300 American and foreign fire helmets on display.

Right:
This 1887 Amoskeag steamer is a 2nd size, 700 gpm. It was originally LAFD Engine 3.

The second floor dormitory at Fire Station 27 was designed to accommodate 30 firemen. This is how the main dorm looked in the 1980's.

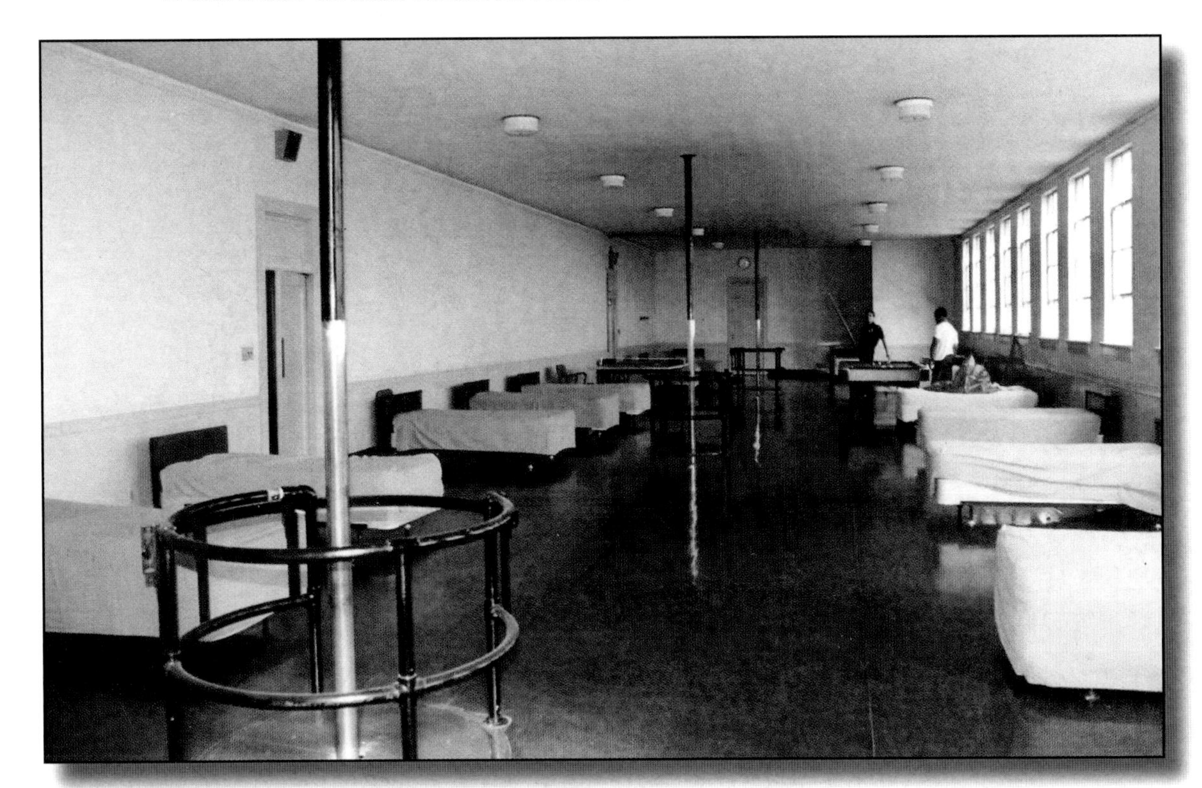

Funds for this 1962 Chevrolet service utility vehicle were donated to the Fire Department by the Mandeville Canyon Property Owners Association as a thank you for saving their homes during the 1961 Bel Air fire. This vehicle is now owned by the Historical Society and assists with activities at the museum.

This 1881 Hayes aerial ladder is the oldest horse drawn apparatus on display. The Hayes was the first practical aerial ladder built. The ladder is raised by a very large hand crank and screw mechanism.

One of two 1954 Cadillac ambulances used by the department is now on display at the museum.

The LAFD Historical Society operates two fire museums in Los Angeles. Besides the main museum in Hollywood, the Historical Society also operates a museum at old Fire Station 36 in the San Pedro area of the harbor. This beautifully restored 1923 Seagrave triple at the museum was actually assigned there for most of its career.

Los Angeles Fallen Firefighters' Memorial Pin.

Structural element from the World Trade Center twin towers form the 9-11 Memorial at the Frank Hotchkin Memorial Training Center in Elysian Park.

Fallen firefighters memorial.

The Museum and Memorial

On August 19, 2004, ground was broken for the fallen firefighters memorial at the museum. Pictured are, from left to right, Council Member Tom LaBonge, the fire chief's wife Liz Bamattre, HS member Isabel Rosas, Fire Chief William Bamattre, and President of United Firefighters of Los Angeles City, Pat McOsker.

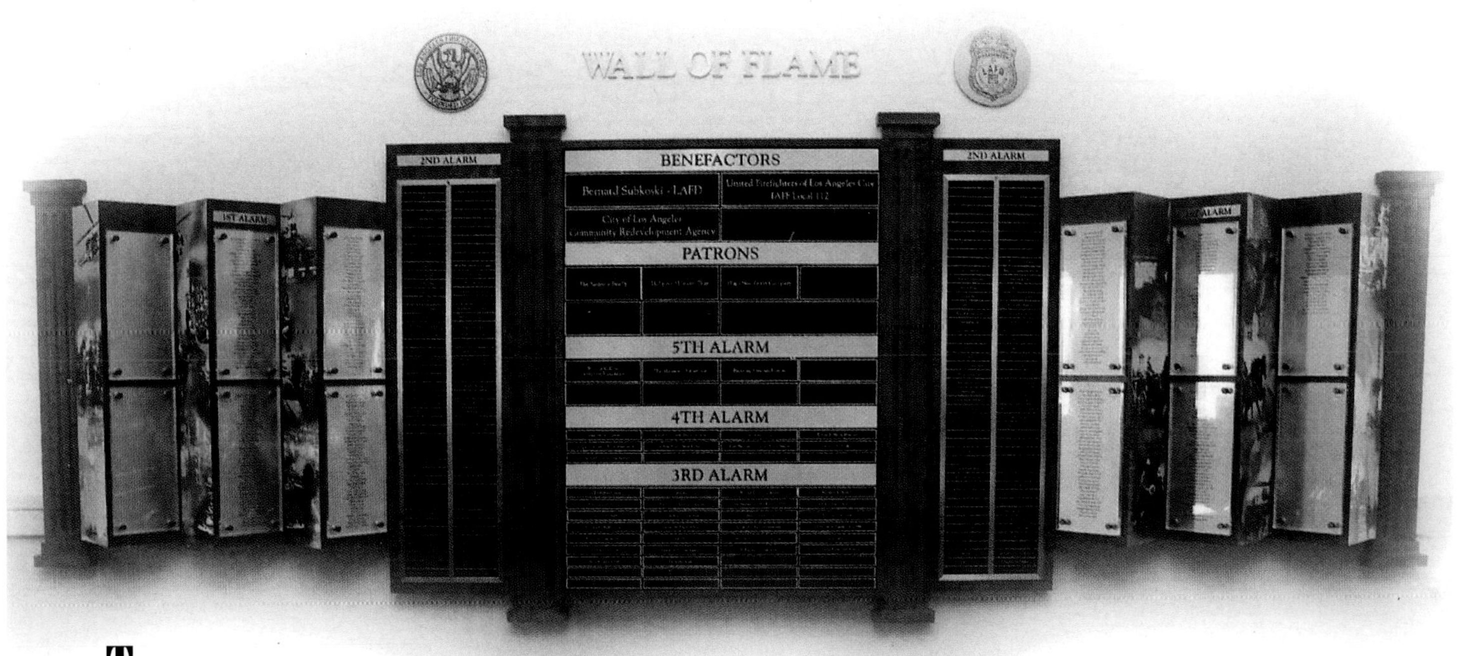

The Wall of Flame in the museum honors those who contribute to the memorial project.

This Cenotaph that stands in front of Los Angeles City Hall was erected in 1944 as a tribute to those fire personnel who died in World War II. Since there was no other suitable memorial to fallen fire fighters, it was used for many years for memorial services for fire fighters who died in the line of duty.

Acknowledgments

While compiling this book, every effort was made to use photos that were not printed in any other publication. However, it is inevitable that one or more photos that were chosen may have been seen somewhere else. As there were hundreds of photos, negatives, and slides available to choose from, it was very difficult to select the photos that depicted the LAFD's rich history while being interesting for the reader to view. We regret that we had to omit so many great photos due to the limited space of this book.

This pictorial history of the Los Angeles Fire Department was made possible through the efforts of the members of the Historical Society and the society's photo archives. We are also grateful to the following photographers and collectors of historic photos who provided the photos that appear in this book. Larry Arnold, J. August, David Blair, Scott Brady, Frank Brown, Hal Burba, Leon Callaway, Claude A. Conlin, Jr., Dave Cox, Adrian Cottrell, Bill Dahlquist, Toni DiDomenico, Paul Ditzel, Brian Dixon, Larry Edwards, Robert Foster, P. Garns, Phil Glickman, Mrs. E. A. Gripp, Ken Gustafson, Xavier Hermosillo, George Homer, W. A. Hughes, Walt Jaeger, Tim Kennoy, Ray Kent, John Lahickey, Cecil R. Lynch, Jr., Chuck Madderom, Dale Magee, Frank Manwarren, D. R. Martin, Phil McBride, Rick McClure, Reid McDonald, Mike Meadows, D. R. Neal, Bud Nelson, Art Rogers, G. M. Roland, Bob Schneller, Mort Schuman, Alan Simmons, Gordon Sommers, John Squire, Title Insurance & Trust Co., Jack Witner, The City Engineers Office, The Port of Los Angeles and the photo archives of the Los Angeles Fire Department.

A special thanks to all the members of the Historical Society, active and retired members of the Los Angeles Fire Department, and friends of the Historical Society Museum who spent many hours selecting photos, providing information, writing and researching photo captions, proof reading, editing text, scanning photos, and other support which made this book possible. These helpers include Ted Aquaro, Liz Bamattre, Frank Borden, Dave Cox, Eric Cox, Bill Dahlquist, Bob DeFeo, Don Dodd, Jennifer Finn, Jim Finn, Greg Gibson, Tim Griffin, Walt Jaeger, Lee Kebler, Tracy Koerner, Tom LeNay, Barney Nipp, Joe Ortiz and Larry Schneider.

We have made every effort to credit the individuals, both living and deceased, who have contributed to this publication. We apologize for any omissions or errors that may have occurred.

Index